dress-to-impress
KNITTED
BOOT CUFFS &
LEG WARMERS

dress-to-impress

KNITTED
BOOT CUFFS &
LEG WARMERS

25
fun to
wear
designs

Pam Powers

STACKPOLE
BOOKS

Guilford, Connecticut

Published by Stackpole Books
An imprint of Globe Pequot
Trade Division of The Rowman & Littlefield Publishing Group, Inc.
4501 Forbes Boulevard, Suite 200, Lanham, Maryland 20706

Distributed by NATIONAL BOOK NETWORK
800-462-6420

Copyright © 2017 Pam Powers
Cover design by Caroline Stover
Project and model photography by Misty Matz
How-to photography by Claire Powers

British Library Cataloguing in Publication Information Available
Library of Congress Cataloging-in-Publication Data Available
ISBN 978-0-8117-1799-1 (paperback)
ISBN 978-0-8117-6579-4 (e-book)

♾™ The paper used in this publication meets the minimum
requirements of American National Standard for Information Sciences—
Permanence of Paper for Printed Library Materials, ANSI/NISO
Z39.48-1992.

First Edition

Printed in the United States of America

Contents

10 Short Boot Liners

Introduction

Knit It/Wear It

There are many different compelling reasons to knit. So much press has been given to the therapeutic benefits of knitting. And the hand-maker movement is moving forward at full speed. Maybe you (like me) learned to knit as a child but then revisited it as an adult as a way to express creativity and have a little "something," a hobby or pastime to do on the side.

These are all great reasons for knitting, but after you experience your warm, fuzzy feeling over "I made this," the next step is to turn knitting into a utilitarian (practical) activity. "How do I do that?" you may be asking yourself. Consider this: You can make accessories that are truly unique and comparable to pricey handmade knits you would buy from an exclusive boutique. You know you are really onto something when people stop asking, "Did you make this?" and instead inquire, "Wherever did you buy this?"

Inspiration for Design

So this is my outlook on knitting: I knit a lot—all the time, nonstop, day and night. And when I'm not knitting, I'm thinking about knitting. I think about what I would like to own and wear but have not seen sold or available as a knitting pattern. This is how the notion of boot liners evolved for me. I wanted a little something decorative to pop out of the top of my boots—not way out, just a few inches to transition (segue) between boot and leg or pants. I tried decorative over-the-knee socks but couldn't find the right weight and design. Plus, they weren't adjustable because of the foot, other than scrunching the tops down with shorter boots.

I did some research and found a few Etsy stores selling finished "boot cuffs." These are 4–5"/10–15 cm knitted cuffs that you strategically position to wear with your boots. They were easy enough to design, so I made a couple of pairs and put them to the test. What I found was that they constantly needed to be adjusted, especially if you sit down, then stand up, because of a tendency to move around on your leg. I then made a version that looked more like a leg warmer that was tapered so it didn't bunch up around your ankles if your boots were on the fitted side.

So Many Options

Sure, you could make a bunch of hand-knitted socks to wear with your boots. But consider this: Feet are usually the hardest part of the sock to make. Good for you if this is not an issue, but for the rest of us, eliminating the foot takes away a lot of measuring and shaping. Also, some of my boots are a little on the tight side, so having a bulky hand-knit foot is not always ideal. Finally, when you take away the foot, you have many more wearing options. Even with the tall boot liners, you do have a little wiggle room in moving them up or down. In this book I give you a lot of options to wear with all different styles of boots and outfits.

Please take the time to read through the pattern completely before beginning a project.

And be sure to check out the "How to Read My Patterns" and "Special Techniques" chapters to make sure you are on the right track.

Let's get started!

How to Read My Patterns

Every designer has her own unique way of presenting her patterns. I have developed this format over the years that I have been designing in response to feedback I have gotten from knitters.

Finished Measurements (and Size/Fit)

These are the measurements of the garment taken after blocking. For more complete measurements, refer to the schematic provided for each project. Remember also that all measurements given within the pattern as you work are blocked measurements as well. For example, if a pattern states "work until piece measures 10"/25.5 cm," this measurement pertains to a blocked knitted fabric. So if your blocked row gauge is 7 rows per inch, but unblocked gauge is 8 rows per inch, you would work 70 rows, even though your piece will measure out at 8¾" unblocked. For this example, your unblocked measurement would be ⅞ of the blocked measurement you are trying to achieve, dividing your blocked gauge by your unblocked gauge.

A note about fit: Boot liners should have a 10–25 percent negative ease. To determine your size, measure around the largest part of the leg that will be covered by the boot liner and subtract 10–25 percent, then find the size that is closest to that measurement. When deciding the final circumference for each boot liner, consider the type of fabric you are creating (i.e., ribbing will have more elasticity than stockinette) and what you may wear under the boot liner—a pair of tights or denim, for example.

I think the easiest way to make a liner smaller is to use a finer gauge yarn. If you want to adapt a pattern, you need to add or subtract stitches based on the repeat of the stitch pattern involved. For example, if the stitch pattern has a 6-stitch repeat, then your stitch count needs to be divisible by 6. Also, all of the boot liners have ribbing on the bottom, so your number of stitches needs to be divisible by 4 when you get to that section. In the case that it is not, you need to either add stitches with increases or subtract with decreases to get to the appropriate stitch count.

Yarn

For each project, I tell you how many yards are required (and for each yarn, if there are multiple colors), so you'll be able to figure out how many skeins you need, no matter what yarns you choose. The particular yarns and colors I used for the project are listed, including their weight, fiber content, and how many yards/meters are in each skein.

Yarn Substitutions

If you decide to use an alternate yarn, there are a number of factors to consider to ensure success. The gauge needs to be within 1 to 2 stitches (taken from a 4" swatch) of the gauge listed for the pattern. However, the weight of the yarn is also an important consideration. Calculate the yards per gram for both the yarn used and for the substitution yarn by dividing the yards per skein by the grams per skein. If there is a large difference (more than 10 percent), then the finished product may have a different drape than the sample shown in the book, which is a problem for patterns that are dependent on a certain degree of substance. Also it's important that the substitute yarn have a fiber content that behaves similarly to that of the original yarns used, as different fibers have varying densities that will perform differently in patterns regardless of the gauge. For example, a wool yarn tends to have a lot of body whereas a cotton or hemp yarn typically will not, so it would not be a good substitution.

Yarn Weights

0 LACE	Fingering, 10-count Crochet Thread
1 SUPER FINE	Sock, Fingering, Baby
2 FINE	Sport, Baby
3 LIGHT	DK, Light Worsted
4 MEDIUM	Worsted, Afghan, Aran
5 BULKY	Chunky, Craft, Rug
6 SUPER BULKY	Super Bulky, Roving
7 JUMBO	Jumbo, Roving

Needles

These are the needle sizes and types used in production of the samples. However, if your gauge does not match the pattern gauge listed (see below for more on that), then you will need to adjust your needle size to obtain the appropriate gauge. If your swatch ends up being too large, move down a needle size, and vice versa. Some patterns have circular needles listed even though the piece is not knitted in the round. This is because either a longer needle is required to accommodate the number of stitches being worked with (or because it is just easier to carry a large number of stitches on circulars) or because you will need to access the knitting from both ends of the needle. In this circumstance, you could use straight needles and transfer the stitches to the second needle in order to work from the other end. If there are not a large number of stitches being worked, you could also use a double-pointed needle.

Most of these designs are worked circularly. Because the circumference of a boot liner is on the smaller side, one circular needle will probably not work unless you are doing the magic loop method. In the specifics for the patterns, I list double-pointed needles (dpns), but this is only a suggestion. Feel free to use whatever method you prefer. My favorite method for making boot liners is working with two sets of circular needles, with half of the stitches placed on each set.

Abbreviations

2/1/2 LPC	Slip 3 stitches to cable needle and hold in front; k2, slip purl stitch from cable needle onto left-hand needle and p1; k2 from cable needle.
2/1/2 RPC	Slip 3 stitches to cable needle and hold in back; k2, slip purl stitch from cable needle onto left-hand needle and p1; k2 from cable needle.
2/2 LC	Slip 2 stitches to cable needle and hold in front; k2; k2 from cable needle.
2/2 LPC	Slip 2 stitches to cable needle and hold in front; p2; k2 from cable needle.
2/2 RC	Slip 2 stitches to cable needle and hold in back; k2; k2 from cable needle.
2/2 RPC	Slip 2 stitches to cable needle and hold in back; k2; p2 from cable needle.
3/3 LC	Slip 3 stitches to cable needle and hold in front; k1, p1, k1; k1, p1, k1 from cable needle.
3/3 RC	Slip 3 stitches to cable needle and hold in back; k1, p1, k1; k1, p1, k1 from cable needle.
approx	approximately
beg	beginning
BO	bind off
Cable YO	Pass 3rd stitch on left-hand needle over the 2nd and 1st stitches; k1, yo, k1.
Cable YOP	Pass 3rd stitch on left-hand needle over the 2nd and 1st stitches; p1, yo, p1.
CC	contrasting color
cdd	central double decrease: Slip 2 stitches as if to knit 2 together, knit 1, pass slipped stitches over.
CL	Cluster: Slip 6 stitches to cable needle; wrap yarn clockwise around stitches on cable needle 3 times; knit the stitches from cable needle.
cm	centimeter
cn	cable needle
CO	cast on
cont	continue
dec	decrease(ing)
g	gram
inc	increase(ing)
k	knit
k1-tbl	Knit 1 stitch through the back loop.
k2tog	Knit 2 stitches together (right-slanting decrease).
kf&b	Knit into front then back of same stitch.
LH	left-hand

m	meter(s)
M1L (M1)	Make 1 Left (Make 1): Insert left-hand needle, from front to back, under strand of yarn that runs between next stitch on left-hand needle and last stitch on right-hand needle; knit this stitch through back loop. 1 stitch increased.
M1P	Make 1 Purl: Insert left-hand needle, from front to back, under strand of yarn that runs between next stitch on left-hand needle and last stitch on right-hand needle; purl this stitch through back loop. 1 stitch increased.
M1R	Make 1 Right: Insert left-hand needle, from back to front, under strand of yarn which runs between next stitch on left-hand needle and last stitch on right-hand needle; knit this stitch through front loop. 1 stitch increased.
MC	main color
p	purl
p2tog	Purl 2 stitches together.
pat(s)	pattern(s)
pm	place marker
rem	remain(ing)
rep	repeat
RH	right-hand
rnd(s)	round(s)
RS	right side(s)
sl m	slip marker
ssk	Slip 2 stitches individually as if to knit, then knit those 2 stitches together though the back loops (left-slanting decrease).
ssp	Slip 2 stitches individually as if to knit, then purl those 2 stitches together though the back loops (left-slanting decrease).
sssk	Slip 3 stitches individually as if to knit, then knit those 3 stitches together though the back loops (left-slanting decrease).
st(s)	stitch(es)
St st	stockinette stitch: Knit on right side rows and purl on wrong side rows.
tog	together
WS	wrong side
wyib	with yarn in back
wyif	with yarn in front
yd(s)	yard(s)
yo	yarn over

Notions

These supplies include such things as stitch markers and holders, tapestry needles, and buttons and other closures.

Gauge

This is the gauge you need to match in order for the finished garment to correspond to the dimensions on the schematic. The gauge is always given for blocked, knitted fabric. Please take the time to knit a gauge swatch. It will help to ensure that your finished cuffs will fit your leg properly. Also, the swatch is where you will determine if the stitches look pleasing. For example, if you need to go up one or more needle sizes in order to achieve the listed gauge, but there are big holes in the stitches caused by the looseness of the fabric, then that yarn is not a good match for the project. Make a good-size swatch (I usually make a 6"/15.5 cm square swatch) and take the time to block it before measuring it.

Level of Difficulty

Patterns are rated with skill levels as defined by the Craft Yarn Council of America, as follows:

Easy—Projects using basic stitches, repetitive stitch patterns, simple color changes, and simple shaping and finishing.

Intermediate—Projects with a variety of stitches, such as basic cables and lace, simple intarsia, double-pointed needles and knitting in the round needle techniques, and mid-level shaping and finishing.

Experienced—Projects using advanced techniques and stitches, such as short rows, Fair Isle, more intricate intarsia, cables, lace patterns, and numerous color changes.

Pattern Notes

This is where any special construction notes are given, such as how the piece is worked (i.e., from the top down, from the center out starting with a provisional cast-on, etc.). Some patterns have special selvage instructions, such as "slip first stitch of every row with yarn in front." Be sure to check for any Pattern Notes before starting the project.

Special Stitches/ Techniques

This is a list of the special stitches or techniques used in the pattern. For instance, there are many different cables used throughout this book. At first glance, many of these cables look similar to each other, but please review here which cables you will be working, paying close attention to make sure you are following the correct instructions.

Pattern Stitches

This is where you will find stitch patterns that are used as a repeat within the instructions. If there is a chart included with the pattern, this is where you will find the row-by-row instructions listed for the corresponding chart. Charts are read from the bottom up and from right to left on right-side rows. Wrong-side rows are read from left to right. The symbols on the chart represent the pattern as you are looking at it from the right side. If knitting in the round, every row is a right-side row. If knitting flat, the symbols need to be reinterpreted for the wrong side; for example, a knit symbol will be purled and a purl symbol will be knit.

Finishing

All garments should be wet blocked. For further instructions, see Tubular Blocking on page 8.

When sewing on buttons or hooks, I always try to use the project yarn and a tapestry needle. Sewing thread has a tendency to cut through yarn over time. However, occasionally it will be necessary to use a sewing needle and thread if the holes of the buttons or hooks are not large enough to pass a tapestry needle through or if the project yarn is bulky. If that is the case, use thread or a finer gauge yarn in a natural, not synthetic, fiber.

Special Techniques

These are techniques used repeatedly in the patterns. Photos are included for further clarification.

Jeny's Surprisingly Stretchy Bind-Off

The bottom cuff of the boot liner needs to have a lot of elasticity in order to be pulled over the foot. There are many different stretchy bind-off methods but I find this one created by Jeny Staiman to have the most give, and as a bonus it is easy to memorize. It's basically a regular bind-off, but each stitch is "processed" with a yarn over to allow a little more give between stitches.

To process a knit stitch:

1. Start with a reverse yarn over—wrap the yarn from the back, over the needle, ending with the yarn in front.

2. Knit 1 stitch.

3. Using the LH needle, slip the yarn over up and over the stitch you just knitted.

To process a purl stitch:

1. Start with a yarn over—wrap the yarn from the front, over the needle, ending with the yarn in back.

2. Purl 1 stitch.

3. Using the LH needle, slip the yarn over up and over the stitch you just purled.

To bind off:

1. After you have 2 processed stitches, knit or purl, on your RH needle . . .

2. Slip the bottom stitch up and over the top stitch and off the needle—1 stitch bound off.

3. Continue processing stitches before binding off, till you get to the last stitch, then pull yarn through that stitch.

Tubular Blocking

In order to get professional-looking finished garments, you need to block, especially with lace patterns in order to open up the yarn overs and see the beauty of the design. With items worked circularly, however, you can't just pin them onto a blocking board. I make custom blocking forms based on the dimensions of the schematic. It's easy to do, and you probably have all of the supplies already in your possession.

For tapered boot liners, cut a piece of cardboard (double it if it's thin) to the following dimensions:
- Top width is half the top circumference of the boot liner minus about ½"/1.25 cm to accommodate for the girth of the plastic wrap.
- Bottom width is half the bottom circumference minus ½"/1.25 cm.
- Add 1"/2.5 cm to the top and bottom.
- Draw a diagonal line from where the tapering starts to the base width.

For straight boot liners, cut a piece of cardboard to the following dimensions:
- Width is half the circumference minus about ½"/1.25 cm
- Height is finished height plus at least 2"/5 cm.

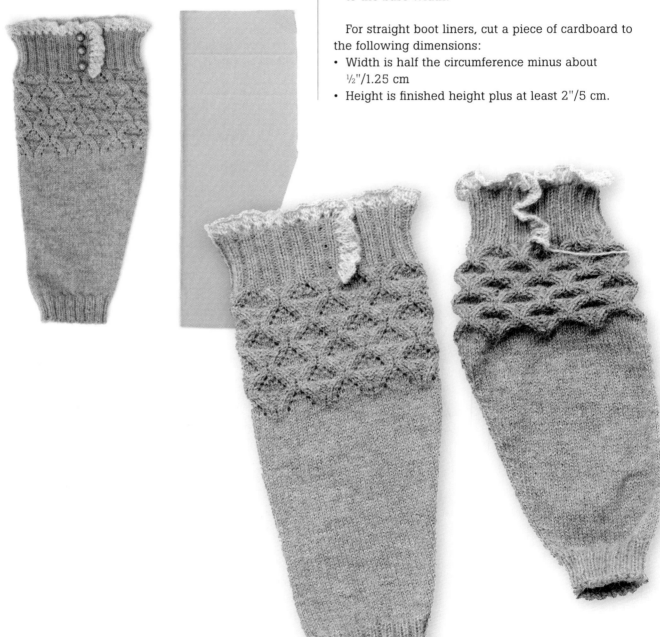

1. Wrap the cardboard with 2 to 3 layers of plastic wrap to waterproof.

Thoroughly soak boot liners in cold water. Gently squeeze out excess water and roll in a towel if necessary.

2. Place boot liner over the form and pin in place if necessary.

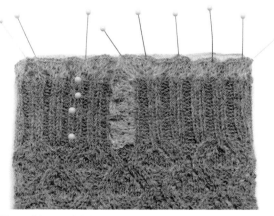

3. If working with lace, pull to open up yarn overs and shape stitch pattern.

Allow to dry completely before removing from form.

If ribbing has become too stretched, you can shrink by simply taking a spray bottle and wetting just the ribbed section. Scrunch and let dry.

Short Boot Liners

Short boot liners have no shaping; they are basically a knitted tube. They are designed to be worn with shorter boots—from booties to mid-calf height.

The short liner is probably the most flexible style of the collection. The patterns in this section could all be adapted to wear more like a cuff with taller boots—just make sure the circumference is the appropriate size for your calf. You could also use any of these patterns for a younger girl to wear with taller boots.

Double
Roll

FINISHED MEASUREMENTS

7"/17.5 cm tall and 8½ (11, 13½)"/21.5 (28, 34.5) cm
circumference

YARN

Color A: 110 (140, 175) yds/101 (128, 160) m light
worsted weight #3 yarn (shown in Natural Mix,
Patons Classic Wool Worsted; 100% wool; 210
yds/192 m per 3.5 oz/100 g skein)

Color B: 45 (60, 75) yds/41 (55, 68.5) m light
worsted weight #3 yarn (shown in Seafoam, Patons
Classic Wool Worsted; 100% wool; 210 yds/192 m
per 3.5 oz/100 g skein)

NEEDLES

❧ US size 4 (3.5 mm), 1 set of double-pointed needles
❧ US size 6 (4.0 mm), 2 sets of double-pointed
   needles or 1 set of double-pointed needles and
   1 circular needle any length (for 3-Needle Join)
*Adjust needle sizes if necessary to obtain
   correct gauge.*

NOTIONS

❧ Tapestry needle
❧ Stitch marker

GAUGE

Using larger needles, 21 sts and 27 rows in St st =
   4"/10 cm square, blocked

LEVEL OF DIFFICULTY

Easy, with added skill of 3-Needle Join

PATTERN NOTES

❧ Worked from the top down in one piece.
❧ Two layers are worked separately, joined together
   using 3-Needle Join, then worked as one layer.
❧ If using one set of double-pointed needles and 1
   circular needle for the join, place B layer stitches
   on circular needle after last round.

SPECIAL TECHNIQUE

3-Needle Join: Holding A Layer in front of B Layer
   with RS of both pieces facing forward and needles
   parallel, using a third needle, knit tog 1 st from the
   front needle with 1 from the back. *Knit tog 1 st
   each from the front and back needles. Rep from *
   around.

PATTERN STITCHES

2 x 2 Rib (multiple of 4 sts)
Pat rnd: *K2, p2; rep from * around.

1 x 1 Rib (multiple of 2 sts)
Pat rnd: *K1, p1; rep from * around.

Boot Liners

B Layer

With B and smaller needles, CO 44 (56, 68) sts. Mark beg of rnd and join, taking care not to twist sts.

Rnds 1–7: Knit.

Change to larger needles.

Rnds 8–9: Work in 1 x 1 Rib.

Rnds 10–13: Knit.

Leave sts on dpns or place on circular needle. Cut B.

A Layer

With A and smaller needles, CO 44 (56, 68) sts. Mark beg of rnd and join, taking care not to twist sts.

Knit for 7 rnds.

Change to larger needles.

Work 2 rnds in 1 x 1 Rib. Do not cut A.

Join Layers

With A and using 3-Needle Join with larger needles, join B Layer to A Layer.

With A and larger needles, knit every rnd until piece measures 6"/15 cm from top edge. Cut A.

Join B, work in 2 x 2 Rib until piece measures 7"/17.5 cm from top edge.

BO using Stretchy BO (see page 6).

Finishing

Weave in ends. Block using Tubular Blocking method (see page 8).

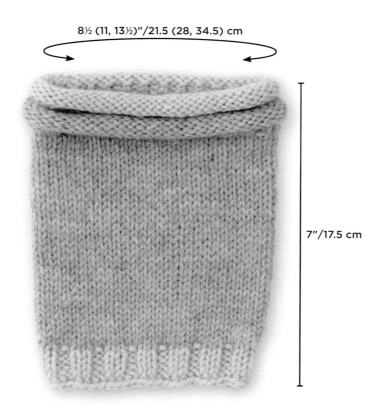

8½ (11, 13½)"/21.5 (28, 34.5) cm

7"/17.5 cm

Fox
River

FINISHED MEASUREMENTS

9"/23 cm tall and 8½ (10, 11½)"/21.5 (25.5, 29) cm top circumference

YARN

Color A: 275 (325, 370) yds/251.5 (297, 338.5) m fingering weight #1 yarn (shown in Beige, Loops & Threads Woolike; 85% acrylic, 15% nylon; 678 yds/620 m per 3.5 oz/100 g skein)

Color B: 45 (55, 65) yds/41 (50.5, 59.5) m fingering weight #1 yarn (shown in Mauve, Loops & Threads Woolike; 85% acrylic, 15% nylon; 678 yds/620 m per 3.5 oz/100 g skein)

Color C: 45 (55, 65) yds/41 (50.5, 59.5) m fingering weight #1 yarn (shown in Charcoal, Loops & Threads Woolike; 85% acrylic, 15% nylon; 678 yds/620 m per 3.5 oz/100 g skein)

Color D: 185 (220, 250) yds/169 (201, 228.5) m fingering weight #1 yarn (shown in Sage, Loops & Threads Woolike; 85% acrylic, 15% nylon; 678 yds/620 m per 3.5 oz/100 g skein)

NEEDLES

☙ US size 2.5 (3 mm), 1 set of double-pointed needles

Adjust needle size if necessary to obtain correct gauge.

NOTIONS

☙ Tapestry needle
☙ Stitch marker

GAUGE

32 sts and 34 rows in 3 x 1 Rib with 2 strands held together = 4"/10 cm square, blocked

LEVEL OF DIFFICULTY

Easy

PATTERN NOTES

☙ Worked from the top down in one piece.
☙ Pattern worked with 2 strands of yarn held together throughout.
☙ When working stripes, do not cut unused strand of A. Twist A and C strands and carry yarn up at beginning of round.

PATTERN STITCHES

2 x 2 Rib (multiple of 4 sts)
Pat rnd: *K2, p2; rep from * around.

3 x 1 Rib (multiple of 4 sts)
Pat rnd: *K3, p1; rep from * around.

Boot Liners

Cuff

With 2 strands of B, CO 68 (80, 92). Mark beg of rnd and join, taking care not to twist sts.

Work 3 rnds in 2 x 2 Rib. Cut both strands of B.

Stripe Section

Join 2 strands of A, work 4 rnds of 3 x 1 Rib. Do not cut either strand of A.

Join 1 strand of C. With 1 strand of A and 1 strand of C, work 4 rnds of 3 x 1 Rib. Do not cut C.

With 2 strands of A, work 4 rnds of 3 x 1 Rib. Do not cut A.

With 1 strand of A and 1 strand of C, work 4 rnds of 3 x 1 Rib. Cut C.

With 2 strands of A, work 5 rnds of 3 x 1 Rib. Cut 1 strand of A.

Body

Join 1 strand of D. With 1 strand of A and 1 strand of D, work 3 x 1 Rib until piece measures 9"/23 cm from CO edge.

BO using Stretchy BO (see page 6).

Finishing

Weave in ends. Block using Tubular Blocking method (see page 8).

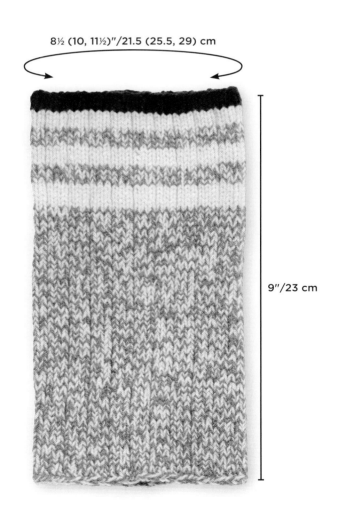

8½ (10, 11½)"/21.5 (25.5, 29) cm

9"/23 cm

Honeycomb

FINISHED MEASUREMENTS

7½"/19 cm tall and 8 (10, 12)"/20.5 (25.5, 30.5) cm top circumference, unstretched

YARN

Color A: 115 (140, 170) yds/105 (128, 155.5) m DK weight #3 yarn (shown in Seagreen Heather or Flagstone, Patons Classic Wool DK Superwash; 100% pure new wool; 125 yds/114 m per 1.8 oz/50 g skein)

Color B: 35 (45, 50) yds/32 (41, 45.5) m DK weight #3 yarn (shown in Aran, Patons Classic Wool DK Superwash; 100% pure new wool; 125 yds/114 m per 1.8 oz/50 g skein)

NEDLES

- US size 4 (3.5 mm), 1 set of double-pointed needles
- US size 5 (3.75 mm), 1 set of double-pointed needles

Adjust needle sizes if necessary to obtain correct gauge.

NOTIONS

- Tapestry needle
- Stitch marker

GAUGE

Using smaller needles, 25½ sts and 61 rows in Slip-Stitch Pat = 4"/10 cm square, blocked.

LEVEL OF DIFFICULTY

Easy

PATTERN NOTES

- Worked from the top down in one piece.
- Slip stitches purlwise with yarn held in back.
- Carry nonworking yarn up at beginning of round by twisting both yarns together.

PATTERN STITCHES

Slip-Stitch Pattern (multiple of 4 sts)

Rnds 1–3: With B, *sl 2, k2; rep from * around.
Rnd 4: With A, knit.
Rnds 5–6: Purl.
Rnds 7–9: With B, *k2, sl 2; rep from * around.
Rnd 10: With A, knit.
Rnds 11–12: Purl.
Rep Rnds 1–12 for pat.

2 x 2 Rib (multiple of 4 sts)
Pat rnd: *K2, p2; rep from * around.

Boot Liners

Using A and with smaller needles, CO 52 (64, 76) sts.
  Mark beg of rnd and join, taking care not to twist
  sts.

Rnds 1–3: Purl. Do not cut A.

Join B.

Rnds 4–5: With B, knit.

Rnd 6: With A, knit.

Change to larger needles.

Rnds 7–8: purl.

Work Rnds 1–12 of Slip-Stitch Pat over 52 (64, 76)
  sts, 4 times over 48 rows. Cut B.

Ribbing

Work even in 2 x 2 Rib until piece measures
  7"/17.5 cm from CO edge.

BO using Stretchy BO (see page 6).

Finishing

Weave in ends. Block using Tubular Blocking method
  (see page 8).

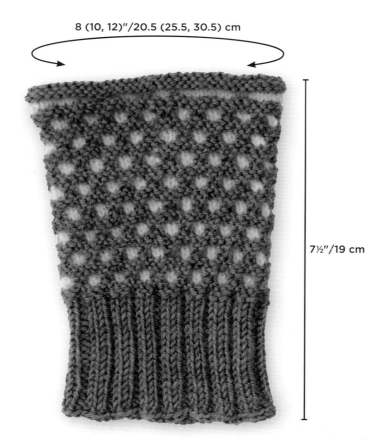

8 (10, 12)"/20.5 (25.5, 30.5) cm

7½"/19 cm

Harley

FINISHED MEASUREMENTS

7"/17.5 cm tall and 9 (11, 13)"/23 (28, 33) cm top circumference

YARN

145 (175, 205) yds/132.5 (160, 187.5) m DK weight #3 yarn (shown in Leopard, Madelinetosh Tosh DK; 100% superwash merino wool; 225 yds/206 m per 3.5 oz/100 g skein)

NEEDLES

❦ US size 4 (3.5 mm), 1 set of double-pointed needles
❦ US size 6 (4 mm), 1 set of double-pointed needles
Adjust needle sizes if necessary to obtain correct gauge.

NOTIONS

❦ Tapestry needle
❦ Stitch marker
❦ ¼" pyramid studs (available at craft stores or online at studsandspikes.com) and small pair of pliers

GAUGE

Using larger needles, 23 sts and 36 rows in Quilted Lattice Pat = 4"/10 cm square, blocked.

LEVEL OF DIFFICULTY

Intermediate

PATTERN NOTES

❦ Worked from the top down in one piece with rolled Stockinette stitch top edge.

PATTERN STITCHES

2 x 2 Rib (multiple of 4 sts)
Pat rnd: *K2, p2; rep from * around.

Quilted Lattice Pattern (multiple of 6 sts)
(See tutorial on page 25.)
Rnd 1: *Sl 5 wyif, k1; rep from * around.
Rnds 2 and 4: Knit.
Rnd 3: K2, *insert RH needle under loose strand and knit next st, bringing new st out from under strand, k5; rep from * to last 4 sts, k1 under loose strand, k3.
Rnd 5: K3, *sl 5 wyif, k1; rep from * to last 3 sts, sl 3 wyif.
Rnd 6: With yarn still in front, sl 2, knit to end.
Rnd 7: *K5, k1 under loose strand; rep from * around.
Rnd 8: Knit.
Rep Rnds 1–8 for pat.

Boot Liners

With smaller needles, CO 52 (64, 76) sts. Mark beg of rnd and join, taking care not to twist sts.

Rnds 1–4: Knit.

Change to larger needles.

Rnds 5–10: Work in 2 x 2 Rib.

Rnd 11: M1, k26 (32, 38), M1, knit to end—54 (66, 78) sts.

Work in Quilted Lattice Pattern until piece measures 5"/13 cm from CO edge, ending with either Rnd 3 or Rnd 7.

Dec rnd: K2tog, k24 (30, 36), k2tog, knit around—52 (64, 76) sts rem.

Work in 2 x 2 Rib until piece measures 7"/17.5 cm from CO edge.

BO using Stretchy BO (see page 6).

Finishing

Weave in ends. Block using Tubular Blocking method (see page 8).

Attach pyramid studs, as follows:

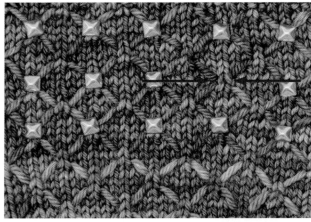

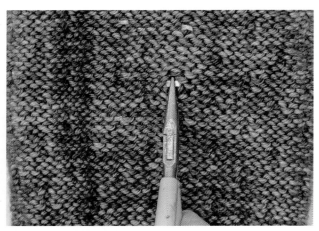

2. On the wrong side bend the prongs in with your pliers, making sure they are securely gripping the yarn.

1. Place stud over cross bar of yarn, making sure the prongs are placed through the opening in the middle of stitches (not splitting the yarn).

9 (11, 13)"/23 (28, 33) cm

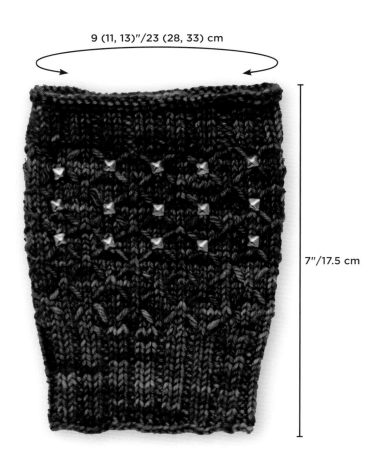

7"/17.5 cm

Quilted Lattice Stitch Pattern Tutorial: How to Work the Loose Strand

1. (Rnd 1) Slip 5 sts with yarn in front, knit 1.

3. (Rnd 3) Knit next stitch.

2. (Rnd 3) Insert RH needle under loose strand and into next stitch on needle.

4. (Rnd 3) Bring new stitch out from under strand.

Bandit

FINISHED MEASUREMENTS

8"/20.5 cm tall and 9 (10½, 12)"/23 (26.5, 30.5) cm
top circumference

YARN

Color A: 70 (85, 95) yds/64 (77.5, 87) m light
worsted weight #3 yarn (shown in Aran, Patons
Classic Wool Worsted; 100% wool; 210 yds/192 m
per 3.5 oz/100 g skein)

Color B: 35 (40, 45) yds/32 (36.5, 41) m light
worsted weight #3 yarn (shown in Dark Grey Marl,
Patons Classic Wool Worsted; 100% wool; 210
yds/192 m per 3.5 oz/100 g skein)

Color C: 40 (45, 50) yds/36.5 (41, 45.5) m light
worsted weight #3 yarn (shown in Black, Patons
Classic Wool Worsted; 100% wool; 210 yds/192 m
per 3.5 oz/100 g skein)

Color D: 20 (25, 25) yds/18.5 (23, 23) m light
worsted weight #3 yarn (shown in Bright Red,
Patons Classic Wool Worsted; 100% wool; 210
yds/192 m per 3.5 oz/100 g skein)

NEEDLES

❦ US size 6 (4 mm), 1 set of double-pointed needles
*Adjust needle size if necessary to obtain
correct gauge.*

NOTIONS

❦ Tapestry needle
❦ Stitch marker

GAUGE

23 sts and 29 rows in Stripe Pat = 4"/10 cm square,
blocked

LEVEL OF DIFFICULTY

Easy

PATTERN NOTES

❦ Worked from the top down in one piece.
❦ When working stripes, twist and carry unused yarn
up at beginning of round.

PATTERN STITCHES

2 x 2 Rib (multiple of 4 sts)
Pat rnd: *K2, p2; rep from * around.

Stripe Pattern
Rnds 1 and 2: With B, knit.
Rnds 3 and 4: With C, knit.
Rnds 5 and 6: With A, knit.
Rnd 7: With D, knit.
Rnds 8 and 9: With A, knit.
Rnds 10 and 11: With C, knit.
Rnds 12 and 13: With B, knit.
With circular knitting, you are actually working in a
spiral, not in even circular layers, so stripes tend to
"jog" where the last stitch of a round does not line
up with the first stitch. For jogless stripes, sl first st
on Rnds 2, 4, 6, 8, and 11.
Rep Rnds 1–13 for pat.

Boot Liners

Ribbed Cuff

With A, CO 52 (60, 68) sts. Mark beg of rnd and join,
taking care not to twist sts.
Work 6 rnds in 2 x 2 Rib.

Pattern Section

Work 4 reps of Stripe Pat over 52 rnds. Cut B, C,
and D.

Ribbed Cuff

With A, work in 2 x 2 Rib for 7 rnds.
BO using Stretchy BO (see page 6).

Finishing

Weave in ends. Block using Tubular Blocking method
(see page 8).

9 (10½, 12)"/23 (26.5, 30.5) cm

8"/20.5 cm

Through
the Woods

FINISHED MEASUREMENTS

8"/20.5 cm tall and 10 (12½, 15)"/25.5 (32, 38) cm circumference

YARN

Color A: 50 (65, 75) yds/45.5 (59.5, 68.5) m worsted weight #4 yarn (shown in #865 Olive Heather, Cascade 220 Superwash; 100% superwash wool; 220 yds/200 m per 3.5 oz/100 g skein)

Color B: 55 (70, 80) yds/50.5 (64, 73) m worsted weight #4 yarn (shown in #1910 Summer Sky Heather, Cascade 220 Superwash; 100% superwash wool; 220 yds/200 m per 3.5 oz/100 g skein)

Color C: 100 (130, 150) yds/91.5 (119, 137) m worsted weight #4 yarn (shown in #862 Walnut Heather, Cascade 220 Superwash; 100% superwash wool; 220 yds/200 m per 3.5 oz/100 g skein)

NEEDLES

✷ US size 6 (4 mm), 1 set of double-pointed needles
Adjust needle size if necessary to obtain correct gauge.

10 (12½, 15)"/25.5 (32, 38) cm

8"/20.5 cm

NOTIONS

✷ Tapestry needle
✷ Stitch marker

GAUGE

26 sts and 32 rows in 2-color stranded St st = 4"/10 cm square, blocked

LEVEL OF DIFFICULTY

Intermediate, with stranding

PATTERN NOTES

✷ Worked from the top down in one piece.
✷ Colorwork is worked using 2-color stranded St st.

PATTERN STITCH

2 x 2 Rib (multiple of 4 sts)
Pat rnd: *K2, p2; rep from * around.

Boot Liners

Using A, CO 64 sts. Mark beg of rnd and join, taking care not to twist sts.

Work 2 rnds in 2 x 2 Rib. Cut A.

Join B, knit 1 rnd.

Work 4 rnds in 2 x 2 Rib.

Knit 4 rnds. Do not cut B.

Join A, complete Color Chart on page 32, knitting all sts in colors as indicated, cutting B at Rnd 14 of chart and joining C at Rnd 15.

With C, work in St st until piece measures 5½"/14 cm.

Work in 2 x 2 Rib until piece measures 7½"/19 cm. Cut C.

Join A, knit 1 rnd.

Work 2 rnds in 2 x 2 Rib.

BO using Stretchy BO (see page 6).

Finishing

Weave in ends. Block using Tubular Blocking method (see page 8).

Two-Color Stranding

Two-color stranding is when two colors are worked simultaneously in one row or round. The color placement is determined by a Color Chart that shows you how many stitches to knit in each color. In the Color Chart on page 32, the trees are upside down because this boot liner is worked from the top down.

When you change colors, the new color yarn is stranded across the back of some number of stitches creating a "float." The tension of the float is very important in stranded knitting. If tension is too tight, your work will pucker, which not only looks bad, but your boot liner may not be stretchy enough to get your foot and leg through. If tension is too loose, you can get snagged on the floats, and the stitches may become large and uneven on the visible side. The correct tension of the floats will be slightly loose but straight and even when the knitting is laid flat.

On the left you see the right side of the cuff with the Color Chart repeat outlined in red. The wrong side of the cuff shows floats knitted with correct tension; they flow straight across, neither stretched nor sagging.

COLOR CHART

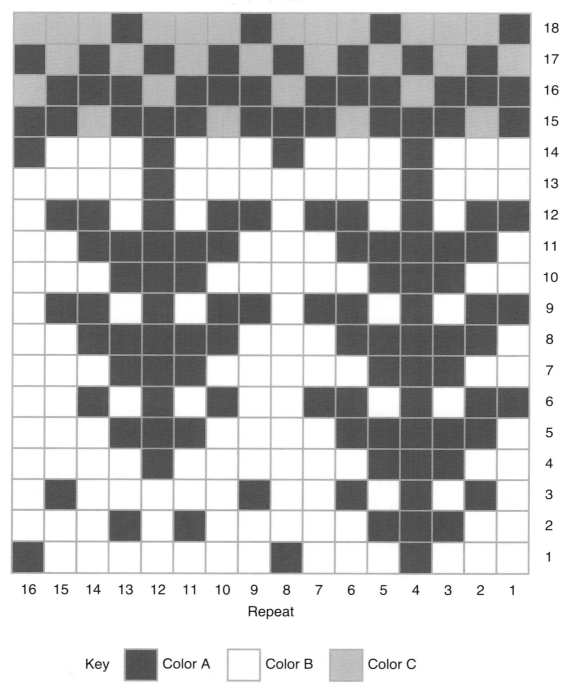

Key ■ Color A □ Color B ■ Color C

Prairie

FINISHED MEASUREMENTS

8½"/21.5 cm tall (not including lace trim) and 9 (10, 11)"/23 (25.5, 28) cm top circumference

YARN

Color A: 140 (155, 175) yds/128 (141.5, 160) m fingering weight #1 yarn (shown in Denim, Madelinetosh Tosh Sock; 100% superwash merino wool; 395 yds/361 m per 4.2 oz/120 g skein)

Color B: 25 (30, 35) yds/23 (27.5, 32) m fingering weight #1 yarn (shown in Paper, Madelinetosh Tosh Sock; 100% superwash merino wool; 395 yds/361 m per 4.2 oz/120 g skein)

NEEDLES

❧ US size 2 (2.75 mm), 1 set of double-pointed needles

❧ US size 3 (3.25 mm), 1 set of double-pointed needles

Adjust needle sizes if necessary to obtain correct gauge.

NOTIONS

❧ Tapestry needle
❧ Stitch marker

GAUGE

Using larger needles, 35½ sts and 38 rnds in Lace Pat = 4"/10 cm square, blocked.

LEVEL OF DIFFICULTY

Intermediate

PATTERN NOTES

❧ Worked from the top down in one piece, starting with lace trim.

SPECIAL TECHNIQUE

Picot Cast-On: *CO 4 sts using knitted CO (for instructions see Step 4 of the Split Heel Tutorial, pages 46–47), BO 2 sts, slip st from RH needle to LH needle; rep from * until desired number of sts are CO.

SPECIAL STITCH

Cable YO: Pass third st on LH needle over the second and first sts; k1, yo, k1.

PATTERN STITCHES

2 x 2 Rib (multiple of 4 sts)
Pat rnd: *K2, p2; rep from * around.

Lace Pattern (multiple of 8 sts)
Rnd 1: *P1, Cable YO, p1, k3; rep from * around.
Rnd 2: *P1, k3; rep from * around.
Rnd 3: *P1, k3, p1, Cable YO; rep from * around.
Rnd 4: Rep Rnd 2.
Rep Rnds 1–4 for pat.

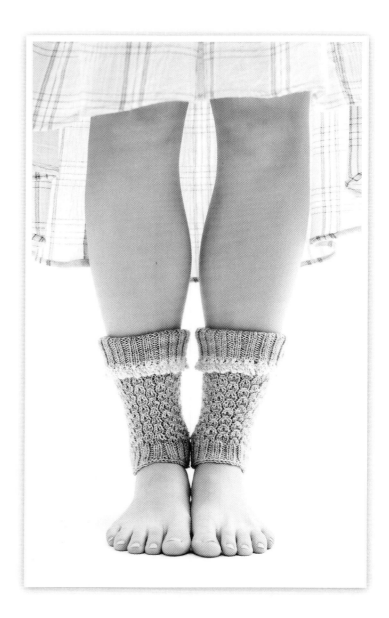

Boot Liners

Lace Trim

Using smaller needles, B, and Picot Cast-On, CO 80 (88, 96) sts. Mark beg of rnd and join, taking care not to twist sts.

Rnd 1: Knit.
Rnd 2: *K2tog, yo; rep from * around.
Rnd 3: Knit.

Ribbing

Using A and larger needles, work in 2 x 2 Rib for 2½"/6.5 cm, measured from top of ribbing.

Lace Section

Work Rnds 1–4 of Lace Pat until piece measures 7"/17.5 cm from top of ribbing, ending on either Rnd 2 or Rnd 4.

Ribbing

Work in 2 x 2 Rib for 1"/2.5 cm. BO using Stretchy BO (see page 6).

Finishing

Weave in ends. Block using Tubular Blocking method (see page 8).

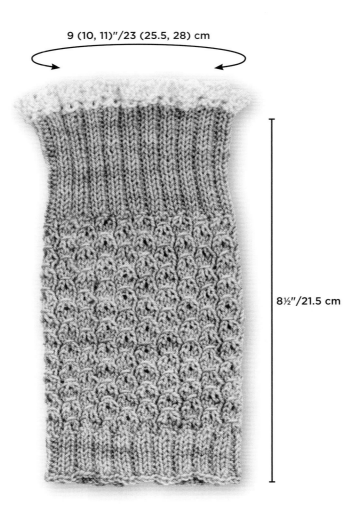

9 (10, 11)"/23 (25.5, 28) cm

8½"/21.5 cm

Torch

FINISHED MEASUREMENTS

10"/25.5 cm tall and 9 (10, 11½)"/23 (25.5, 29) cm
  top circumference

YARN

Color A: 140 (155, 175) yds/128 (141.5, 160) m sport
  weight #2 yarn (shown in #507 Gray and #505
  Beige, Blue Sky Alpaca Sport Weight; 100% baby
  alpaca; 110 yds/100 m per 1.8 oz/50 g skein)
Color B: 65 (75, 85) yds/59.5 (68.5, 77.5) m sport
  weight #2 yarn (shown in #807 gold and #806
  Salsa, Blue Sky Alpaca Melange; 100% baby
  alpaca; 110 yds/100 m per 1.8 oz/50 g skein)

NEEDLES

❦ US size 4 (3.5 mm), 1 set of double-pointed needles
*Adjust needle size if necessary to obtain
  correct gauge.*

NOTIONS

❦ Tapestry needle
❦ Stitch marker

GAUGE

32 sts and 25 rows in Twisted-Stitch Lace Pat =
  4"/10 cm square, blocked
24 sts and 31 rows in Eyelet Pat = 4"/10 cm square,
  blocked

LEVEL OF DIFFICULTY

Experienced

PATTERN NOTES

❦ Worked from the top down in one piece.

PATTERN STITCHES

2 x 2 Rib (multiple of 4 sts)
Pat rnd: *K2, p2; rep from * around.

Twisted-Stitch Lace Pattern (multiple of 10 sts)
Rnd 1: *Yo, ssk, [p1, k1-tbl] 4 times; rep from *
  around.
Rnd 2: *Yo, p1, ssk, [k1-tbl, p1] 3 times, k1-tbl; rep
  from * around.

(continued on page 39)

Rnd 3: *Yo, k1-tbl, p1, ssk, [p1, k1-tbl] 3 times; rep from * around.

Rnd 4: *Yo, p1, k1-tbl, p1, ssk, [k1-tbl, p1] twice, k1-tbl; rep from * around.

Rnd 5: *Yo, [k1-tbl, p1] twice, ssk, [p1, k1-tbl] twice; rep from * around.

Rnd 6: *Yo, [p1, k1-tbl] twice, p1, ssk, k1-tbl, p1, k1-tbl; rep from * around.

Rnd 7: *Yo, [k1-tbl, p1] 3 times, ssk, p1, k1-tbl; rep from * around.

Rnd 8: *Yo, [p1, k1-tbl] 3 times, p1, ssk, k1-tbl; rep from * around.

Rnd 9: *Yo, [k1-tbl, p1] 4 times, ssk; rep from * around.

Rnd 10: *Ssk, [p1, k1-tbl] 4 times, yo; rep from * around.

Rnd 11: *Ssk, [k1-tbl, p1] 3 times, k1-tbl, yo, p1; rep from * around.

Rnd 12: *Ssk, [p1, k1-tbl] 3 times, yo, k1-tbl, p1; rep from * around.

Rnd 13: *Ssk, [k1-tbl, p1] twice, k1-tbl, yo, p1, k1-tbl, p1; rep from * around.

Rnd 14: *Ssk, [p1, k1-tbl] twice, yo, [k1-tbl, p1] twice; rep from * around.

Rnd 15: *Ssk, k1-tbl, p1, k1-tbl, yo, [p1, k1-tbl] twice, p1; rep from * around.

Rnd 16: *Ssk, p1, k1-tbl, yo, [k1-tbl, p1] 3 times; rep from * around.

Rnd 17: *Ssk, k1-tbl, yo, [p1, k1-tbl] 3 times, p1; rep from * around.

Rnd 18: *Ssk, yo, [k1-tbl, p1] 4 times; rep from * around.

Eyelet Pattern (multiple of 10 sts)
Rnd 1: Knit.
Rnd 2 and all even rnds: Knit.
Rnd 3: *K1, k2tog, yo, k7; rep from * around.
Rnd 5: *[K2tog, yo] twice, k6; rep from * around.
Rnd 7: Rep Rnd 3.
Rnd 9: Knit.
Rnd 11: *K6, k2tog, yo, k2; rep from * around.
Rnd 13: *K5, [k2tog, yo] twice, k1; rep from * around.
Rnd 15: Rep Rnd 11.
Rnd 16: Knit.
Rep Rnds 1–16 for pat.

Boot Liners

Lace Section
With B, CO 70 (80, 90) sts. Mark beg of rnd and join, taking care not to twist sts.
Work Rnds 1–18 of Twisted-Stitch Lace Pat. Cut B.

Eyelet Section
Join A, knit 1 rnd.
Small size only:
Dec rnd: *K2, k2tog, k1, k2tog; rep from * around—50 sts rem.
Medium size only:
Dec rnd: *K2, k2tog; rep from * around—60 sts rem.
Large size only:
Dec rnd: *K2, k2tog, k3, k2tog; rep from * around—70 sts rem.
All sizes:
Work Rnds 1–16 of Eyelet Pat, 3 times over 48 rnds.

Ribbing
Work in 2 x 2 Rib until ribbing measures 1"/2.5 cm.
BO using Stretchy BO (see page 6).

Finishing

Weave in ends. Block using Tubular Blocking method (see page 8).

9 (10, 11½)"/23 (25.5, 29) cm

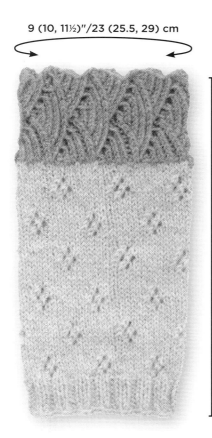

10"/25.5 cm

EYELET PATTERN

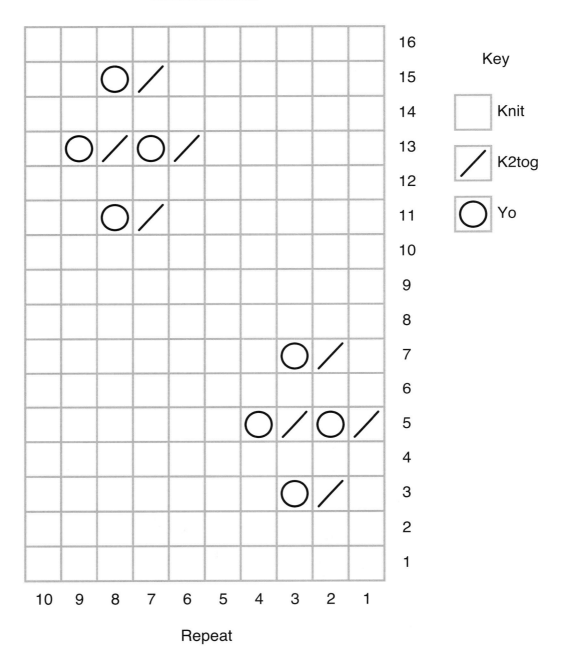

Key

Knit

K2tog

Yo

Repeat

TWISTED-STITCH LACE PATTERN

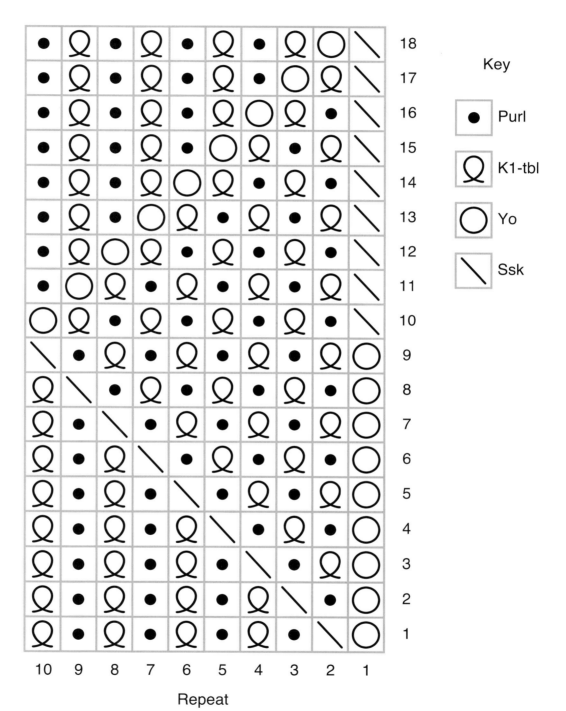

Key

- ● Purl
- Ϙ K1-tbl
- ◯ Yo
- ╲ Ssk

Mary
Jane

FINISHED MEASUREMENTS

7½"/19 cm tall and 8 (9½, 10½)"/20.5 (24, 26.5) cm top circumference

YARN

160 (190, 210) yds/147 (174, 192) m fingering weight #1 yarn (shown in Black Plum, SweetGeorgia Tough Love Sock; 80% superwash merino wool, 20% nylon; 425 yds/388 m per 4.1 oz/115 g skein)

NEEDLES

❦ US size 2 (2.75 mm), 1 set of double-pointed needles
❦ US size 5 (3.75 mm) circular or straight needles (used only for casting on stitches)
Adjust needle sizes if necessary to obtain correct gauge.

NOTIONS

❦ Tapestry needle
❦ Stitch marker

GAUGE

38 sts and 45 rnds in 2 x 2 Rib = 4"/10 cm square, blocked and unstretched
30 sts and 50 rnds in Lace Pat = 4"/10 cm square, blocked

LEVEL OF DIFFICULTY

Intermediate

PATTERN NOTES

❦ Worked in one piece from the bottom up.
❦ Split heel worked by binding off stitches mid-round, then casting on stitches in following round.

SPECIAL STITCH

Cdd (central double decrease): Slip 2 sts as if to knit 2 together, knit 1, pass slipped sts over.

PATTERN STITCHES

2 x 2 Rib (multiple of 4 sts)
Pat rnd: *K2, p2; rep from * around.

Lace Pattern (multiple of 10 sts)
Rnd 1: *[Yo, ssk] twice, k1, [k2tog, yo] twice, k1; rep from * around.
Rnd 2: Knit.
Rnd 3: *K1, yo, ssk, yo, cdd, yo, k2tog, yo, k2; rep from * around.
Rnd 4: Knit.
Rep Rnds 1–4 for pat.

Boot Liners

Ribbed Foot

With larger needles, CO 52 (60, 72) sts. Change to smaller dpns, with sts evenly distributed. Mark beg of rnd and join, taking care not to twist sts.
Work in 2 x 2 Rib until piece measures 3"/7.5 cm.

Split Heel (See tutorial on pages 46–47.)

Heel BO rnd: Work 21 sts in rib, BO 24 (28, 32) sts using Stretchy BO (see page 6), work in rib around.
Heel CO rnd: Work 21 sts in rib, turn; using knitted CO, CO 34 (38, 42) sts, turn; work in rib around—62 (70, 82) sts.
Next rnd: Work 20 sts in rib, ssk, k1, p2, work 28 sts in rib, k1, k2tog, p2, work in rib around—60 (68, 80) sts.

Leg

Work 10 rnds in 2 x 2 Rib.
Medium size only:
Next rnd: M1, k34, M1, knit around—70 sts.
Small and large sizes only:
Next rnd: Knit.
All sizes:
Next 28 rnds: Work 7 reps of Lace Pat.

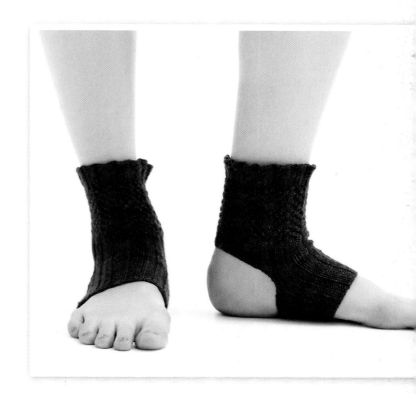

LACE PATTERN

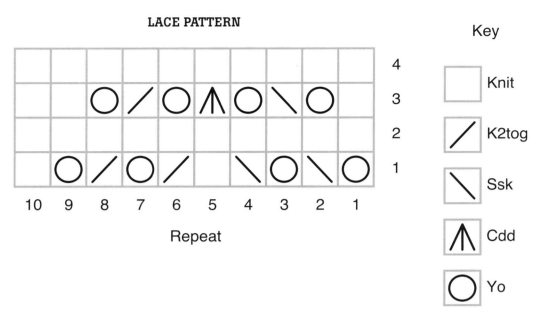

Repeat

Key

□	Knit
╱	K2tog
╲	Ssk
⋀	Cdd
○	Yo

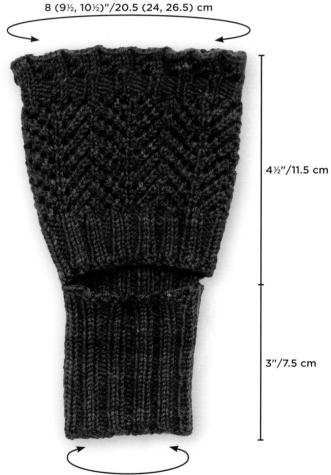

8 (9½, 10½)"/20.5 (24, 26.5) cm

4½"/11.5 cm

3"/7.5 cm

5½ (6½, 7½)"/14 (16.5, 19) cm

Medium size only:
Next rnd: K2tog, k33, k2tog, knit around—68 sts.
Small and large sizes only:
Next rnd: Knit.

Lace Edging
All sizes:
Rnds 1–4: *[K1-tbl] twice, [p1-tbl] twice; rep from * around.
Rnd 5: *K2, yo, p2; rep from * around—75 (85, 100) sts.
Rnd 6: *K3, p2; rep from * around.
Rnd 7: *K3, yo, p2; rep from * around—90 (102, 120) sts.
Rnd 8: *K4, p2; rep from * around.
Rnd 9: *K4, yo, p2; rep from * around—105 (119, 140) sts.
Rnd 10: *K5, p2; rep from * around.
BO all sts loosely in pat.

Finishing

Weave in ends. Block using Tubular Blocking method (see page 8).

Split Heel Tutorial

Sometimes shorter boot liners have a tendency to move around, so a split heel adds a little stability by having that extra band of fabric around the foot. If this process is going to cause you stress, you can always eliminate the split heel altogether—cast-on 60 (68, 80) sts, and begin at the Leg section. Also, if you need to wear the liner up higher on your leg, just pull the foot portion up onto your ankle. This tutorial is taken from the smallest size of the Mary Jane short boot liners, but it is the same technique used for all of the split heel patterns throughout the book.

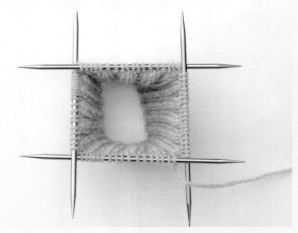

1. Work in 2 x 2 Rib until piece measures 3"/7.5 cm.

3. Heel CO Rnd: Work 21 sts in rib, turn.

2. Heel BO Rnd: Work 21 sts in rib, BO 24 sts using Stretchy BO (see page 6), work in rib around.

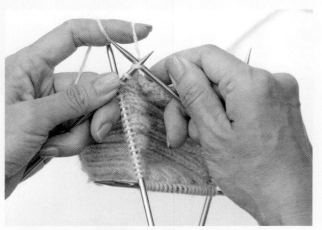

4. Work the knitted CO as follows:
Insert the RH needle into the st and wrap as if to knit.

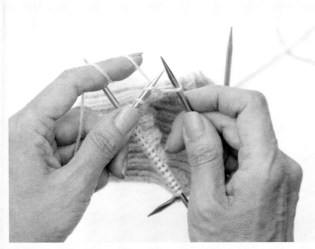

Pull the wrap through.

6. Turn; work in rib around—62 sts.

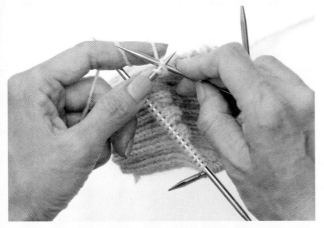

Slip the new st onto the LH needle purlwise.

7. Next rnd: Work 20 sts in rib, ssk, k1, p2, work 28 sts in rib, k1, k2tog, p2, work in rib around—60 sts.

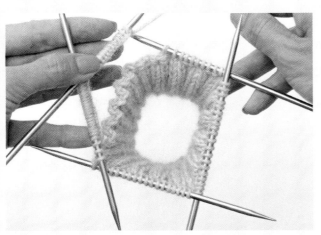

5. CO 34 sts.

Tall Boot Liners

These boot liners are designed to be worn with taller boots, from mid-calf height all the way up to over-the-knee varieties. These long boot liners differ from leg warmers in that they are tapered to the ankle, so they hug your leg and do not "bag" around the ankle. This enables you to wear tighter fitting boots comfortably with the liners.

I tried to incorporate design elements to make these boot liners real statement pieces. In my opinion, a "statement piece" is an eye-catching accessory that takes an outfit from ordinary to head-turning. Wear your favorite jeans, sweater, and boots, but add a band of braided cables with delicate buttons up the side peeking out of the top of the boots—now that's worth a second look! Go ahead, be adventurous! Pick a design that truly reflects your signature style.

Night
and
Day
Mosaic

FINISHED MEASUREMENTS

15"/38 cm tall and 12½ (14½, 16½)"/32 (37, 42) cm top circumference

YARN

Color A: 205 (235, 270) yds/187.5 (215, 247) m chunky weight #5 yarn (shown in #402 Wheat, Lion Brand Wool-Ease Chunky; 86% acrylic, 10% wool, 5% other; 153 yds/140 m per 4.9 oz/140 g skein)

Color B: 10 (15, 15) yds/9 (13.5, 13.5) m chunky weight #5 yarn (shown in #173 Willow, Lion Brand Wool-Ease Chunky; 86% acrylic, 10% wool, 5% other; 153 yds/140 m per 4.9 oz/140 g skein)

Color C: 10 (15, 15) yds/9 (13.5, 13.5) m chunky weight #5 yarn (shown in #144 Eggplant, Lion Brand Wool-Ease Chunky; 86% acrylic, 10% wool, 5% other; 153 yds/140 m per 4.9 oz/140 g skein)

Color D: 10 (15, 15) yds/9 (13.5, 13.5) m chunky weight #5 yarn (shown in #152 Charcoal, Lion Brand Wool-Ease Chunky; 86% acrylic, 10% wool, 5% other; 153 yds/140 m per 4.9 oz/140 g skein)

NEEDLES

❧ US size 9 (5.5 mm), 1 set of double-pointed needles

Adjust needle size if necessary to obtain correct gauge.

NOTIONS

❧ Tapestry needle
❧ Stitch marker

GAUGE

16½ sts and 30 rnds in Night and Day Mosaic Pat = 4"/10 cm square, blocked

16 sts and 23 rnds in St st = 4"/10 cm square, blocked

LEVEL OF DIFFICULTY

Easy

PATTERN NOTES

❧ Worked from the top down in one piece.
❧ The color pattern is formed using slipped stitches—only one color is used per round.

PATTERN STITCHES

2 x 2 Rib (multiple of 4 sts)

Pat rnd: *K2, p2; rep from * around.

Night and Day Mosaic Pattern (multiple of 4 sts)

Note: CC = Color B, C, or D, as indicated in instructions.

Rnd 1: With A, knit.
Rnds 2 and 3: With CC, *sl 2, k2 rep from * around.
Rnds 4 and 5: With A, knit.
Rnds 6 and 7: With CC, knit.
Rnds 8 and 9: With A, *k2, sl 2; rep from * around.
Rnds 10 and 11: With CC, knit.
Rnd 12: With A, knit.
Rep Rnds 1–12 for pat.

Boot Liners

Ribbed Cuff

Using A, CO 52 (60, 68) sts. Mark beg of rnd and join, taking care not to twist sts.

Work 5 rnds in 2 x 2 Rib.

Do not cut A.

Mosaic Section

Rnds 1–12: Work Night and Day Mosaic Pat using B as CC. Cut B.

Rnds 13–24: Work Night and Day Mosaic Pat using C as CC. Cut C.

Rnds 25–36: Work Night and Day Mosaic Pat using D as CC. Cut D.

Leg

With A, knit 2 rnds.

Dec rnd: K1, ssk, knit to last 2 sts, k2tog—2 sts dec'd.

Cont working in St st, rep Dec rnd every 4 (3, 3) rnds 7 (5, 5) more times, then every 5 (4, 4) rnds 2 (6, 6) times—32 (36, 44) sts rem.

Work in St st until piece measures 14"/35.5 cm from CO edge.

Work 7 rnds in 2 x 2 Rib.

BO using Stretchy BO (see page 6).

Finishing

Weave in ends. Block using Tubular Blocking method (see page 8).

NIGHT AND DAY MOSAIC PATTERN

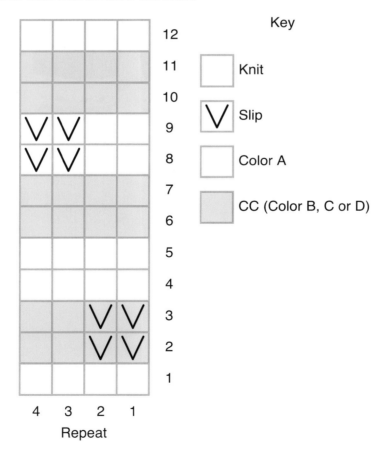

Key

Knit

V Slip

Color A

CC (Color B, C or D)

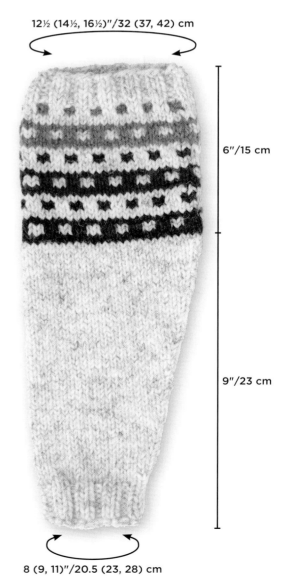

12½ (14½, 16½)"/32 (37, 42) cm

6"/15 cm

9"/23 cm

8 (9, 11)"/20.5 (23, 28) cm

Ashley

FINISHED MEASUREMENTS

12½"/32 cm tall and 12 (13½, 15½)"/30.5 (34.5, 39.5) cm circumference

YARN

215 (245, 280) yds/196.5 (224, 256) m worsted weight #4 yarn (shown in #123 Seaspray, Lion Brand Wool-Ease; 80% acrylic, 20% wool; 197 yds/180 m per 4 oz/85 g skein)

NEEDLES

❧ US 7 (4.5 mm), 1 set of double-pointed needles
Adjust needle size if necessary to obtain correct gauge.

NOTIONS

❧ Tapestry needle
❧ Stitch marker

GAUGE

21 sts and 23½ rows in Lace Pat = 4"/10 cm square, blocked
23 sts and 30 rows in St st = 4"/10 cm square, blocked

LEVEL OF DIFFICULTY

Intermediate

PATTERN NOTES

❧ Worked from the top down in one piece.

PATTERN STITCHES

2 x 2 Rib (multiple of 4 sts)
Pat rnd: *K2, p2; rep from * around.

Lace Pattern (multiple of 9 sts)
Rnd 1: Knit.
Rnd 2: *K1, yo, k2, ssk, k2tog, k2, yo; rep from * around.
Rnd 3: Knit.
Rnd 4: *Yo, k2, ssk, k2tog, k2, yo, k1; rep from * around.
Rep Rnds 1–4 for pat.

Boot Liners

CO 63 (72, 81) sts. Mark beg of rnd and join, taking care not to twist sts.

Rnd 1: Purl.
Rnd 2: Knit.
Rnd 3: *K2tog, yo; rep from * to last st, k1.
Rnd 4: Knit.
Rnd 5: Purl.
Rnds 6–37: Work 7 (8, 9) reps of Lace Pat over 32 rnds.
Rnds 38–40: Knit.
Dec rnd: K1, ssk, knit to last 2 sts, k2tog—2 sts dec'd.
Cont working in St st, rep Dec rnd every 4 (3, 3) rnds 7 (5, 5) more times, then every 5 (4, 4) rnds 1 (6, 6) times—45 (48, 57) sts rem.

LACE PATTERN

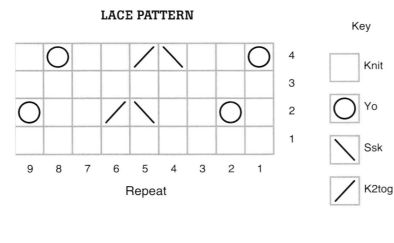

	4
	3
	2
	1

9 8 7 6 5 4 3 2 1

Repeat

Key

☐ Knit

○ Yo

╲ Ssk

╱ K2tog

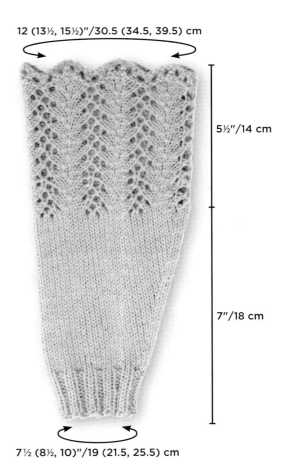

12 (13½, 15½)"/30.5 (34.5, 39.5) cm

5½"/14 cm

7"/18 cm

7½ (8½, 10)"/19 (21.5, 25.5) cm

Small and large sizes only:
Next rnd: K1, ssk, knit around—44 (56) sts rem.
All sizes:
Work in St st until piece measures 11"/28 cm from
   CO edge.
Work 12 rnds in 2 x 2 Rib.
BO using Stretchy BO (see page 6).

Finishing

Weave in ends. Block using Tubular Blocking method
   (see page 8).

Chloe

FINISHED MEASUREMENTS

14½"/37 cm tall and 10 (13, 16)"/25.5 (33, 40.5) cm top circumference, unstretched

YARN

365 (475, 585) yds/334 (434.5, 535) m DK weight #3 yarn (shown in Aran, Patons Classic Wool DK Superwash; 100% pure new wool; 125 yds/114 m per 1.8 oz/50 g skein)

NEEDLES

✤ US size 4 (3.5 mm), 1 set of double-pointed needles
Adjust needle size if necessary to obtain correct gauge.

NOTIONS

✤ Tapestry needle
✤ Stitch markers
✤ Cable needle

GAUGE

33½ sts and 35 rows in Cable Pat = 4"/10 cm, blocked and unstretched
34 sts and 26 rows in 2 x 2 Rib = 4"/10 cm, blocked and unstretched

LEVEL OF DIFFICULTY

Experienced

PATTERN NOTES

✤ Worked from the top down in one piece.

PATTERN STITCHES

2 x 2 Rib (multiple of 4 sts)
Pat rnd: K1, *[p2, k2]; rep from * to last 3 sts, p2, k1; rep from * around.

Single Cable (6 sts)
Rnds 1 and 2: Knit.
Rnd 3: 3/3 LC.
Rnds 4–6: Knit.
Rep Rnds 1–6 for pat.

Double Cable (12 sts)
Rnds 1 and 2: Knit.
Rnd 3: 3/3 R/C, 3/3 LC.
Rnds 4–8: Knit.
Rnd 9: 3/3 LC, 3/3 R/C.
Rnds 10–12: Knit.
Rep Rnds 1–12 for pat.

Boot Liners

Cuff

CO 84 (108, 136) sts. Mark beg of rnd and join, taking
   care not to twist sts.
Work in 2 x 2 Rib until piece measures 3"/7.5 cm from
   CO edge.

Leg

Small size only:
Rnd 1: *K1, p1, work Single Cable over 6 sts, p1,
   work Double Cable twice over 24 sts, p1, work
   Single Cable over 6 sts, p1, k1; rep from * around.
Medium size only:
Rnd 1: *K1, p1, work Single Cable over 6 sts, p1,
   work Double Cable 3 times over 36 sts, p1, work
   Single Cable over 6 sts, p1, k1; rep from * around.
Large size only:
Rnd 1: *K1, p1, [work Single Cable over 6 sts, p1]
   twice, work Double Cable 3 times over 36 sts, p1,
   [work Single Cable over 6 sts, p1] twice, k1; rep
   from * around.

All sizes:
Rnds 2–48: Cont in pat as established, working Rnds
   1–6 of Single Cable chart a total of 8 times and
   Rnds 1–12 of Double Cable chart a total of 4 times.
Rnds 49–53: Work Rnds 1–5 of all charts within
   established pat.

Shape Leg

Rnd 54: K1, [p2, k2] 10 times, pm, k2, pm, [k2, p2]
   10 times, k1.
Dec rnd: Work sts as they present themselves to 2 sts
   before first marker, ssk, sl m, k2, sl m, k2tog, work
   sts as they present themselves to end of rnd—2 sts
   dec'd.
Cont to work in pat as established, working Dec rnd
   every other rnd 16 (19, 25) more times—50 (68, 84)
   sts rem.
Work even until piece measures 14½"/37 cm from CO
   edge.
BO using Stretchy BO (see page 6).

Finishing

Weave in ends. Block using Tubular Blocking method
   (see page 8).

SINGLE CABLE

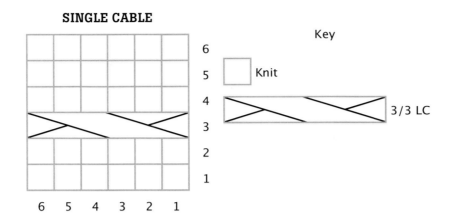

Key

Knit

3/3 LC

DOUBLE CABLE

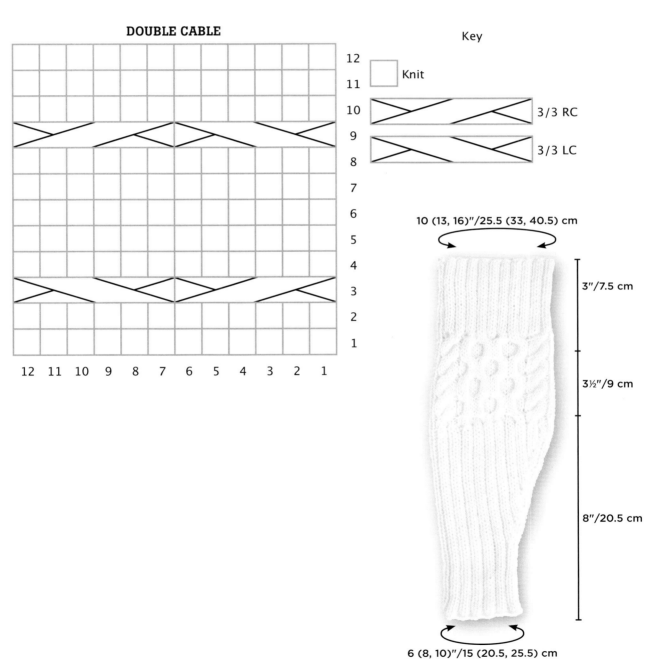

Key

Knit

3/3 RC

3/3 LC

10 (13, 16)"/25.5 (33, 40.5) cm

3"/7.5 cm

3½"/9 cm

8"/20.5 cm

6 (8, 10)"/15 (20.5, 25.5) cm

Gingham
and
Stitch

FINISHED MEASUREMENTS

14½"/37 cm tall and 11½ (13, 14½)"/29 (33, 37) cm top circumference

YARN

Color A: 245 (275, 310) yds/224 (251.5, 283.5) m DK weight #3 yarn (shown in Aran, Patons Classic Wool DK Superwash; 100% pure new wool; 125 yds/114 m per 1.8 oz/50 g skein)

Color B: 110 (125, 140) yds/100.5 (114.5, 128) m DK weight #3 yarn (shown in Denim Heather, Patons Classic Wool DK Superwash; 100% pure new wool; 125 yds/114 m per 1.8 oz/50 g skein)

Color C: 25 (30, 35) yds/23 (27.5, 32) m DK weight #3 yarn (shown in Gold, Patons Classic Wool DK Superwash; 100% pure new wool; 125 yds/114 m per 1.8 oz/50 g skein)

NEEDLES

❧ US size 4 (3.5 mm), 1 set of double-pointed needles
Adjust needle size if necessary to obtain correct gauge.

NOTIONS

❧ Tapestry needle
❧ Stitch marker

GAUGE

23 sts and 28 rows in St st = 4"/10 cm square, blocked

28 sts and 26 rows in 2-color stranded St st = 4"/10 cm square, blocked

LEVEL OF DIFFICULTY

Intermediate, with 2-color stranding (see page 31)

PATTERN NOTES

❧ Worked from the top down in one piece.
❧ Slip stitches purlwise with yarn held in back.
❧ Carry nonworking yarn up at beginning of round by twisting all yarns together.

SPECIAL TECHNIQUE

Slip 2 (sl 2): Slip 2 sts, one at a time, purlwise with the yarn held in back.

PATTERN STITCH

2 x 2 Rib (multiple of 4 sts)
Pat rnd: *K2, p2; rep from * around.

Boot Liners

Ribbed Cuff

Using B, CO 80 (88, 100) sts. Mark beg of rnd and
join, taking care not to twist sts.
Work 7 rnds in 2 x 2 Rib. Do not cut B.

Colorwork Section

Join A, knit for 2 rnds. Do not cut A.
Next rnd: Join C, *k2, sl 2; rep from * around.
Next rnd: *P2, sl 2; rep from * around. Cut C.
Medium size only:
Inc rnd: With A, k1, M1, knit to last st, M1, k1—90 sts.
Small and large sizes only:
Next rnd: Knit.
All sizes:
Work Rnds 1–10 of Color Chart over 80 (90, 100) sts,
knitting all sts in colors as indicated, 3 times over
30 rnds. Cut B.
With A, knit for 1 rnd.

Medium size only:
Dec rnd: K1, ssk, knit to last 2 sts, k2tog—88 sts.
Small and large sizes only:
Next rnd: Knit.
All sizes:
Next rnd: Join C, *k2, sl 2; rep from * around.
Next rnd: *P2, sl 2; rep from * around. Cut C.

Leg

Worked in A only.
Small and medium sizes only:
Set-up rnd: K1, ssk, [k10, k2tog] 6 (7) times, knit to
last 2 sts, k2tog—72 (81) sts rem.
Large size only:
Set-up rnd: K1, ssk, [k9, k2tog] 8 times, knit to last
2 sts, k2tog—90 sts rem.
All sizes:
Knit 2 rnds.
Dec rnd: K1, ssk, knit to last 2 sts, k2tog—2 sts dec'd.
Cont working in St st, rep Dec rnd every 3 rnds 3
(3, 7) more times, then every 4 (4, 4) rnds 7 (7, 4)
times—58 (68, 76) sts rem.

COLOR CHART

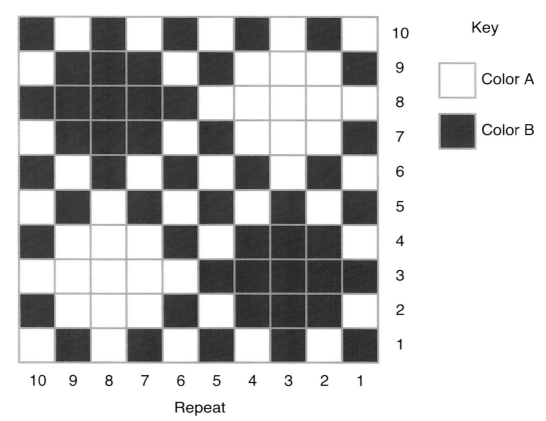

10 9 8 7 6 5 4 3 2 1

Repeat

Key

☐ Color A

■ Color B

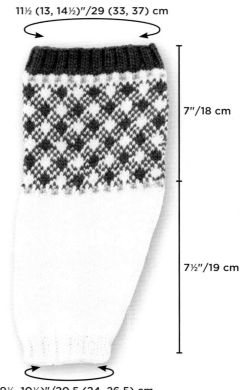

11½ (13, 14½)"/29 (33, 37) cm

7"/18 cm

7½"/19 cm

8 (9½, 10½)"/20.5 (24, 26.5) cm

Work even until piece measures 13"/33 cm from
  CO edge.
Work in 2 x 2 Rib until piece measures 14½"/37 cm
  from CO edge.
BO using Stretchy BO (see page 6).

Finishing

Weave in ends. Block using Tubular Blocking
  method (see page 8).

Claire

FINISHED MEASUREMENTS

18"/46 cm tall (measured with cuff unfolded) and 12 ½ (15, 17 ½)"/32 (38, 44.5) cm cuff edge circumference

YARN

475 (570, 660) yds/434.5 (521, 603.5) m fingering weight #1 yarn (shown in #001 Hare, Rowan Fine Art; 45% wool, 20% mohair, 25% polyamide, 10% silk; 437 yds/400 m per 3.5 oz/100 g skein)

NEEDLES

❦ US size 2 (2.75 mm), 1 set of double-pointed needles or 2 circular needles, any length
Adjust needle size if necessary to obtain correct gauge.

NOTIONS

❦ Tapestry needle
❦ Stitch markers

GAUGE

29 sts and 31 rows in Lace Pat = 4"/10 cm square, blocked
40 sts and 34 rows in Eyelet Rib Pat = 4"/10 cm square, blocked

LEVEL OF DIFFICULTY

Experienced

PATTERN NOTES

❦ Worked from the top down in one piece.
❦ Lace cuff worked first, which will be folded down when worn.
❦ Leg is worked wrong side out.

SPECIAL STITCHES

Sssk: Sl 3 sts individually as if to knit, then knit those 3 sts together through the back loops; left-slanting dec—2 sts dec'd.
Cable YO: Pass third st on LH needle over the second and first sts; k1, yo, k1.
Cable YOP: Pass third st on LH needle over the second and first sts; p1, yo, p1.
Ssp: Slip 2 stitches individually as if to knit, then purl those 2 stitches together though the back loops (left-slanting decrease).

PATTERN STITCHES

2 x 2 Rib (multiple of 4 sts)

Pat rnd: *K2, p2; rep from * around.

Lace Pattern (multiple of 18 sts)

Rnd 1: *P1, k3, p1, k13; rep from * around.
Rnd 2: *P1, Cable YO, p1, yo, k2, ssk, p5, k2tog, k2, yo; rep from * around.
Rnd 3: *P1, k3, p1, k4, p5, k4; rep from * around.
Rnd 4: *P1, k3, p1, k1, yo, k2, ssk, p3, k2tog, k2, yo, k1; rep from * around.
Rnd 5: *P1, k3, p1, k5, p3, k5; rep from * around.
Rnd 6: *P1, Cable YO, p1, k2, yo, k2, ssk, p1, k2tog, k2, yo, k2; rep from * around.
Rnd 7: *P1, k3, [p1, k6] twice; rep from * around.
Rnd 8: *[P1, k3] twice, yo, k2, sssk, k2, yo, k3; rep from * around.

(continued on page 66)

Rnd 9: Rep Rnd 1.
Rnd 10: *P1, Cable YO, p1, k13; rep from * around.
Rnd 11: Rep Rnd 1.
Rnd 12: *P1, k3, p1, yo, k2, ssk, p5, k2tog, k2, yo; rep from * around.
Rnd 13: Rep Rnd 3.
Rnd 14: *P1, Cable YO, p1, k1, yo, k2, ssk, p3, k2tog, k2, yo, k1; rep from * around.
Rnd 15: Rep Rnd 5.
Rnd 16: *P1, k3, p1, k2, yo, k2, ssk, p1, k2tog, k2, yo, k2; rep from * around.
Rnd 17: Rep Rnd 7.
Rnd 18: *P1, Cable YO, p1, k3, yo, k2, sssk, k2, yo, k3; rep from * around.
Rnds 19–20: Rep Rnd 1.
Rep Rnds 1–20 for pat.
Eyelet Rib Pattern (multiple of 9 sts)
Rnd 1: *K1, Cable YOP, k1, p4; rep from * around.
Rnds 2–4: *K1, p3, k1, p4; rep from * around.
Rep Rnds 1–4 for pat.

Boot Liners

Lace Fold-Down Cuff

CO 90 (108, 126) sts. Mark beg of rnd and join, taking care not to twist sts.
Rnd 1: Purl.
Rnd 2: Knit.
Rnd 3: *Yo, k2tog; rep from * around.
Rnd 4: *K1, k1-tbl; rep from * around.
Rnd 5: Purl.
Work Rnds 1–20 of Lace Pat over 90 (108, 126) sts.
Work Rnds 1–11 of Lace Pat.

Ribbing

Rnd 1: *K1, p3, k2, p2, k1; rep from * around.
Rep Rnd 1 until Ribbing section measures 1½"/4 cm.

Leg

Work in Eyelet Rib Pat for 2"/5 cm, ending on Rnd 1.
Set-up rnd: Work in pat for 38 sts, pm, work in pat to end.
Dec rnd: Work in pat to 2 sts before marker, p2tog, sl m, p1, ssp, work in pat to end—2 sts dec'd.
Cont working in Eyelet Rib pat, working Dec rnd every 7 (6, 5) rnds, 4 (9, 5) more times, then every 8 (0, 6) rnds 4 (0, 5) times—72 (88, 104) sts rem.
Work even in pat until leg measures 11"/28 cm from beg of Eyelet Rib section of leg.

Ribbed Cuff

Work in 2 x 2 Rib for 1½"/4 cm.
BO using Stretchy BO (see page 6).

Finishing

Weave in ends. Block using Tubular Blocking method (see page 8).

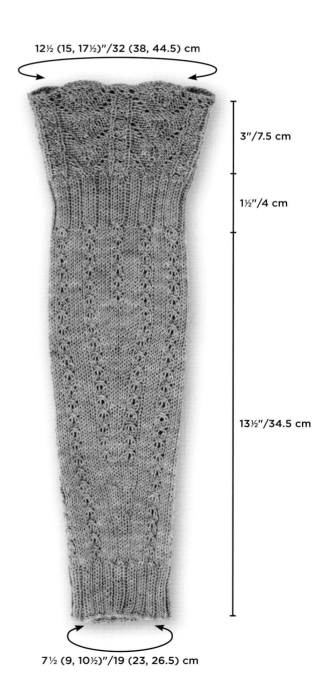

12½ (15, 17½)"/32 (38, 44.5) cm

3"/7.5 cm

1½"/4 cm

13½"/34.5 cm

7½ (9, 10½)"/19 (23, 26.5) cm

LACE PATTERN

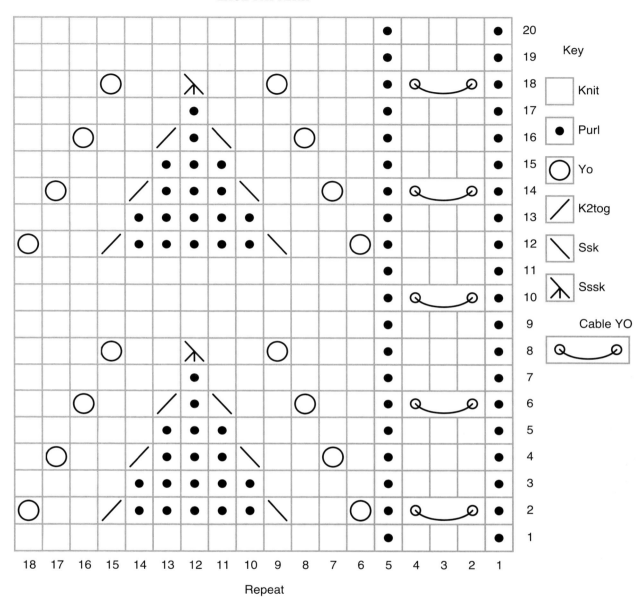

Repeat

Key

- ☐ Knit
- • Purl
- ◯ Yo
- ╱ K2tog
- ╲ Ssk
- ⅄ Sssk

Cable YO

EYELET RIB PATTERN

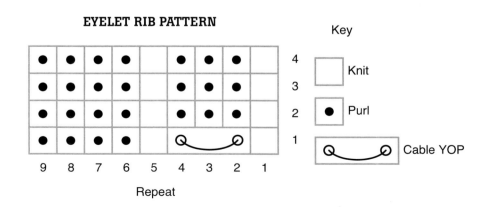

Repeat

Key

- ☐ Knit
- • Purl
- Cable YOP

Jewel

FINISHED MEASUREMENTS

12"/30.5 cm tall and 12½ (15, 17)"/31.5 (38, 43) cm top circumference

YARN

300 (355, 405) yds/274.5 (324.5, 370.5) m light worsted weight #3 yarn (shown in #889 Khaki Sage, Rowan Kid Classic; 70% wool, 22% mohair, 8% polyamide; 140 yds/153 m per 1.8 oz/50 g skein)

NEEDLES

⚜ US size 3 (3.25 mm), straight needles (small)
⚜ US size 4 (3.5 mm), 1 set of double-pointed needles (medium)
⚜ US size 6 (4 mm), straight needles (large)
Adjust needle sizes if necessary to obtain correct gauge.

NOTIONS

⚜ Tapestry needle
⚜ Stitch markers
⚜ Cable needle
⚜ Ten ⅜" buttons
⚜ Sewing needle and thread

GAUGE

Using medium needles, 24 sts and 32 rows in St st = 4"/10 cm square, blocked.
Using large needles, 64 sts and 28 rows in Braided Cable Pat = 4"/10 cm square, blocked.

LEVEL OF DIFFICULTY

Experienced

PATTERN NOTES

⚜ Cabled cuff is knit flat, horizontally, with button placket at cast-on end.
⚜ Leg is worked vertically by picking up stitches from side edge of the cabled cuff.
⚜ Cuff is sewn closed with the bound-off end attached right under the button placket.
⚜ Right and left boot liners have button placket opening in opposite directions, so instructions are different for each side.

SPECIAL STITCHES

2/1/2 RPC: Sl 3 sts to cable needle (cn) and hold in back; k2, sl purl st from cn on to LH needle and p1; k2 from cn.
2/1/2 LPC: Sl 3 sts to cable needle (cn) and hold in front; k2, sl purl st from cn on to LH needle and p1; k2 from cn.

PATTERN STITCHES

2 x 2 Rib (multiple of 4 sts)
Pat rnd: *K2, p2; rep from * around.

Braided Cable Pattern (worked flat over 26 sts)
Row 1 (RS): *K2, p1; rep from * to last 2 sts, k2.
Row 2 and all WS rows: *P2, k1; rep from * to last 2 sts, p2.
Row 3: K2, [p1, 2/1/2 LPC] 4 times.
Row 5: Rep Row 1.
Row 7: [2/1/2 RPC, p1] 4 times, k2.
Row 8: Rep Row 2.
Rep Rows 1–8 for pat.

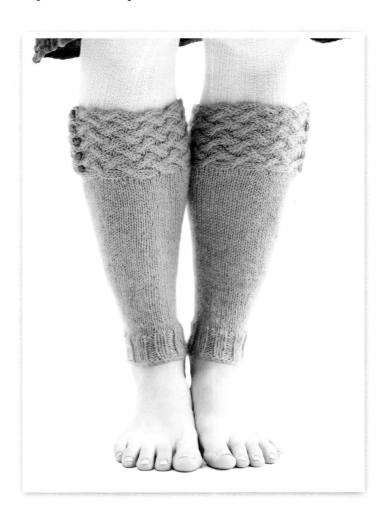

Boot Liners

Button Placket (make 2)

With small straight needles, CO 52 sts.

Row 1 (RS): K2, *k1, slip st just worked from RH needle back to LH needle purlwise, with RH needle lift next 7 sts one at a time over this st and off of needle, yo, knit the first st again, k2; rep from * —22 sts rem.

Row 2: K1, *p2tog, [k1, p1, k1] in yo, p1; rep from * to last st, k1—27 sts rem.

Row 3: Knit.

Cable Pattern

Right boot liner only:

Change to large straight needles.

Set-up row (WS): Work Row 8 of Braided Cable Pat, p1—place marker through last st.

Row 1 (RS): K1, work Row 1 of Braided Cable Pat.

Row 2: Work Row 2 of Braided Cable Pat, p1.

Cont working Braided Cable Pat with 1-st Stockinette selvage on RH side as established.

Work 11 (13, 15) reps of Braided Cable Pat, or until cuff measures approx 12½ (15, 17)"/31.5 (38, 43) cm, measured from marker, ending on Row 8.

BO in pat.

Left boot liner only:

Change to large straight needles.

Set-up row (WS): P1, work Row 8 of Braided Cable Pat—place marker through first st.

Row 1 (RS): Work Row 1 of Braided Cable Pat, k1.

Row 2: P1, work Row 2 of Braided Cable Pat.

Cont working Braided Cable Pat with 1-st Stockinette selvage on LH side as established.

Work 11 (13, 15) reps of Braided Cable Pat, or until cuff measures approx 12½ (15, 17)"/31.5 (38, 43) cm, measured from marker, ending on Row 8.

BO in pat.

Sew cuff closed into a tube using whipstitch, lining up BO edge with marker.

Leg

Right boot liner only:

With RS facing, starting at marker, using medium dpns, pick up and knit 72 (88, 100) sts between selvage st and first st, along edge of cuff, ending at BO end.

Mark beg of rnd and join.

Set-up rnd: Knit, place marker after 52 (64, 73) sts from beg of rnd.

Left boot liner only:

With RS facing, starting at BO end, using medium dpns, pick up and knit 72 (88, 100) sts between selvage st and first st, along edge of cuff, ending at marker.

Mark beg of rnd and join.

Set-up rnd: Knit, place marker after 20 (23, 26) sts from beg of rnd.

Both right and left boot liners:

Knit for 2 rnds.

Dec rnd: Knit to 2 sts before first marker, k2tog, sl m, k1, ssk, knit to end—2 sts dec'd.

Cont in St st and rep Dec rnd every 4 (3, 3) rnds 13 (15, 15) more times, then every 0 (4, 4) rnds 0 (2, 2) times—44 (52, 64) sts rem.

Work even until leg measures 7½"/19 cm from pick-up line.

Ribbed Cuff

Work in 2 x 2 Rib for 1½"/4 cm.

BO using Stretchy BO (see page 6).

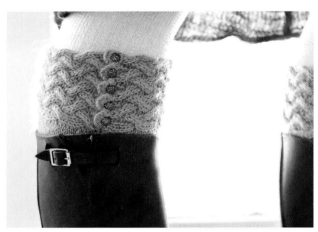

Finishing

Sew buttons in place, referring to photo for placement.

Weave in ends. Block using Tubular Blocking method (see page 8).

BRAIDED CABLE PATTERN

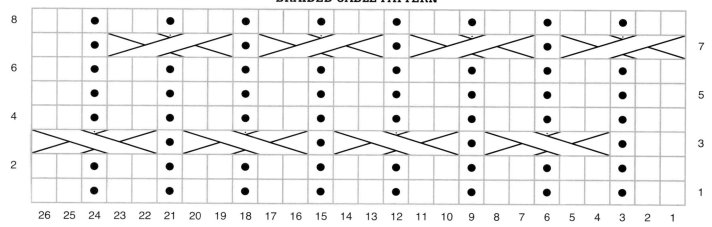

Key

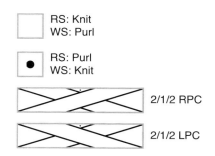

RS: Knit
WS: Purl

RS: Purl
WS: Knit

2/1/2 RPC

2/1/2 LPC

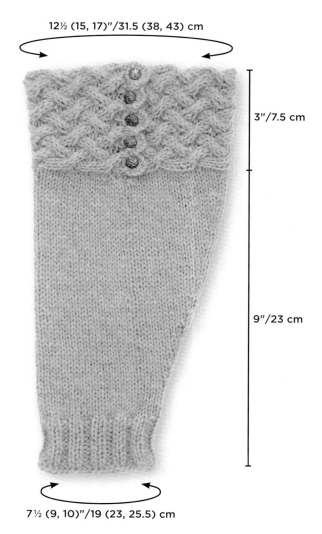

12½ (15, 17)"/31.5 (38, 43) cm

3"/7.5 cm

9"/23 cm

7½ (9, 10)"/19 (23, 25.5) cm

Heidi

FINISHED MEASUREMENTS

19"/48.5 cm tall and 12½ (16, 18)"/32 (40.5, 45.5) cm top circumference (slouchy lace); 11 (14, 15½)"/28 (35.5, 39.5) cm top leg circumference (ribbing and colorwork), unstretched

YARN

Color A: 170 (220, 240) yds/155.5 (201, 219.5) m fingering weight #1 yarn (shown in Raw White, Big Bad Wool Pea Weepaca; 50% fine washable merino, 50% baby alpaca; 175 yds/160 m per 1.8 oz/50 g skein)

Color B: 240 (305, 340) yds/219.5 (279, 311) m fingering weight #1 yarn (shown in Linen, Big Bad Wool Pea Weepaca; 50% fine washable merino, 50% baby alpaca; 175 yds/160 m per 1.8 oz/50 g skein)

Color C: 10 (10, 15) yds/9 (9, 13.5) m fingering weight #1 yarn (shown in Coral, Big Bad Wool Pea Weepaca; 50% fine washable merino, 50% baby alpaca; 175 yds/160 m per 1.8 oz/50 g skein)

Color D: 10 (10, 15) yds/9 (9, 13.5) m fingering weight #1 yarn (shown in Blue Eyes, Big Bad Wool Pea Weepaca; 50% fine washable merino, 50% baby alpaca; 175 yds/160 m per 1.8 oz/50 g skein)

NEEDLES

❦ US size 2 (2.75 mm), 1 set of double-pointed needles (small)

❦ US size 3 (3.25 mm), 1 set of double-pointed needles (medium)

❦ US size 4 (3.5 mm), 1 set of double-pointed needles (large)

Adjust needle sizes if necessary to obtain correct gauge.

NOTIONS

❦ Tapestry needle

❦ Stitch marker

GAUGE

Using medium needles, 31 sts and 41 rows in St st = 4"/10 cm square, blocked.

Using medium needles, 27 sts and 50 rows in Mesh Lace = 4"/10 cm square, blocked.

Using large needles, 31 sts and 44 rows in 2-color stranded St st = 4"/10 cm square, blocked.

LEVEL OF DIFFICULTY

Intermediate

PATTERN NOTES
❧ Boot Liners are knit in the round from the top down in one piece.
❧ There is a rolled St st top followed by Mesh Lace and colorwork done using 2-color stranded St st.
❧ Carry nonworking yarn up at beginning of color rounds by twisting yarns together.

PATTERN STITCHES
3 x 1 Rib (multiple of 4 sts)
Pat rnd: *K3, p1; rep from * around.

2 x 2 Rib (multiple of 4 sts)
Pat rnd: *K2, p2; rep from * around.

Mesh Lace (multiple of 2 sts)
Rnd 1: *Yo, k2tog; rep from * around.
Rnd 2: Knit.
Rnds 3–10: Rep Rnds 1 and 2.
Rnd 11: *Ssk, yo; rep from * around.
Rnd 12: Knit.
Rnds 13–20: Rep Rnds 11 and 12.
Rep Rnds 1–20 for pat.

Boot Liners

Mesh Lace Cuff
Using A and medium needles, CO 84 (108, 120) sts. Mark beg of rnd and join, taking care not to twist sts.
Rnds 1–6: Knit.
Change to small needles.
Rnds 7–46: Work 2 reps of Mesh Lace.
Rnds 47–56: Work Rnds 1–10 of Mesh Lace. Do not cut A.

Ribbing and Colorwork
Change to medium needles and join B, knit 1 rnd.
With B, work 3 rnds of 3 x1 Rib. Do not cut B.
Join C, work 1 rnd of 3 x 1 Rib.
With B, work 2 rnds of 3 x 1 Rib.
With C, work 1 rnd of 3 x 1 Rib.
With B, work 4 rnds of 3 x1 Rib.
Change to large needles and join D.
Work 19 rnds of Color Chart, knitting all sts in colors as indicated. Cut A, C, and D.

Leg

Using B and medium needles, knit 2 rnds.

Dec rnd: K1, ssk, knit to last 2 sts, k2tog—2 sts dec'd.

Cont working in St st, rep Dec rnd every 8 (5, 5) rnds
3 (3, 3) more times, then every 9 (6, 6) rnds 8 (14,
14) times—60 (72, 84) sts rem.

Work even until section that starts with B measures
13"/33 cm from top of Leg ribbing. Cut B.

Join A, knit 1 rnd.

Work 13 rnds of 2 x 2 Rib. Cut A.

Join D, knit 1 rnd.

Work 2 rnds of 2 x 2 Rib.

BO using Stretchy BO (see page 6).

Finishing

Weave in ends. Block using Tubular Blocking method
(see page 8).

COLOR CHART

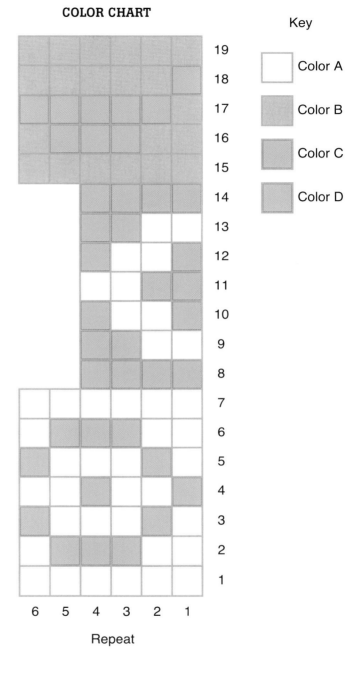

Key

- Color A
- Color B
- Color C
- Color D

Repeat

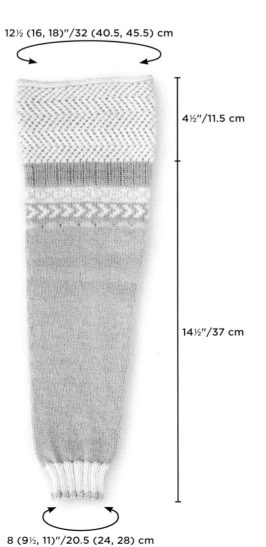

12½ (16, 18)"/32 (40.5, 45.5) cm

4½"/11.5 cm

14½"/37 cm

8 (9½, 11)"/20.5 (24, 28) cm

Lace
and
Button

FINISHED MEASUREMENTS

13"/33 cm tall and 11 (12½, 15)"/28 (32, 38) cm top
circumference

YARN

Color A: 360 (410, 500) yds/330 (375, 457) m
fingering weight #1 yarn (shown in Amethyst
Heather, Cloudborn Baby Alpaca Fingering; 100%
baby alpaca; 201 yds/184 m per 1.8 oz/50 g skein)

Color B: 20 (25, 30) yds/19 (23, 28) m fingering
weight #1 yarn (shown in Grey Heather, Cloudborn
Baby Alpaca Fingering; 100% baby alpaca; 201
yds/184 m per 1.8 oz/50 g skein)

NEEDLES

❦ US size 2 (2.75 mm), 1 set of double-pointed
needles and circular needle for working top lace
edging/faux placket

*Adjust needle size if necessary to obtain
correct gauge.*

NOTIONS

❦ Tapestry needle
❦ Stitch markers
❦ Six ⅜" buttons
❦ Sewing needle and thread

GAUGE

34 sts and 45 rows in St st = 4"/10 cm square,
blocked

35 sts and 51 rows in Lace Pat = 4"/10 cm, blocked

LEVEL OF DIFFICULTY

Intermediate

PATTERN NOTES

❦ Worked from the top down in one piece.
❦ Lace is worked by picking up sts along top edge
and then down ribbed cuff to form faux placket.
❦ Left and right liners mirror each other with the faux
placket positioned at the outside calf.

PATTERN STITCHES

2 x 2 Rib (multiple of 4 sts)
Pat rnd: *K2, p2; rep from * around.

Lace Pattern (multiple of 12 sts)
Rnd 1: *K3, p7, k2; rep from * around.
Rnd 2: *K1, yo, k1, ssk, p5, k2tog, k1, yo; rep from *
around.

Rnd 3: *K4, p5, k3; rep from * around.
Rnd 4: *K2, yo, k1, ssk, p3, k2tog, k1, yo, k1; rep
from * around.
Rnd 5: *K5, p3, k4; rep from * around.
Rnd 6: *K3, yo, k1, ssk, p1, k2tog, k1, yo, k2; rep from
* around.
Rnds 7 and 8: *K6, p1, k5; rep from * around.
Rnd 9: *P4, k5, p3; rep from * around.
Rnd 10: *P3, k2tog, [k1, yo] twice, k1, ssk, p2; rep
from * around.
Rnd 11: *P3, k7, p2; rep from * around.
Rnd 12: *P2, k2tog, k1, yo, k3, yo, k1, ssk, p1; rep
from * around.
Rnd 13: *P2, k9, p1; rep from * around.
Rnd 14: *P1, k2tog, k1, yo, k5, yo, k1, ssk; rep from *
around.
Rnds 15 and 16: *P1, k11; rep from * around.
Rep Rnds 1–16 for pat.

Boot Liners

Ribbed Cuff

Using A, CO 96 (108, 132) sts. Mark beg of rnd and
join, taking care not to twist sts.

Right liner only:
Place marker-A in 73rd (81st, 101st) st.

Left liner only:
Place marker-A in 25th (29th, 33rd) st.

Both liners:
Work 19 rnds of 2 x 2 Rib.

Right liner only:
Place marker-B in 73rd (81st, 101st) st.

Left liner only:
Place marker-B in 25th (29th, 33rd) st.

Lace Section

Both liners:
Knit 1 rnd.
Work 3 complete reps of Lace Pat.
Knit 1 rnd.
Dec rnd: *K1, ssk, knit to last 2 sts, k2tog—2 sts dec.
Cont working in St st, rep Dec rnd every 3 (3, 2) rnds
4 (12, 4) times, then every 4 (4, 3) rnds 13 (7, 19)
times—60 (68, 84) sts rem.
Work even until piece measures 11"/28 cm from CO
edge.
Work 12 rnds in 2 x 2 Rib.
BO using Stretchy BO (see page 6).

Lace Edging and Faux Placket

Right liner only (see tutorial on pages 80–81):
Top Lace Edging (worked horizontally)
Starting 1 st to the left of marker-A on CO edge and
using B, pick up and knit 71 (81, 99) sts (approx 3
sts for every 4 sts) around, ending with last st at
marker-A. Pm between last st and next-to-last st.

Faux Placket Lace (worked vertically)
In column of sts between marker-A and marker-B,
pick up and knit 15 sts (3 sts for every 4 rows),
ending with last st at marker-B. Pm between first
and second sts of 15 just picked up.

Left liner only:
Faux Placket Lace (worked vertically)
Starting at marker-B and using B, pick up and knit
15 sts (3 sts for every 4 rows) in column of sts
between marker-A and marker-B, ending with last
st in st below marker-B. Pm between last st and
next-to-last st.

Top Lace Edging (worked horizontally)
Starting at marker-A on CO edge, pick up and knit 71
(81, 99) sts (approx 3 sts for every 4 sts) around,
ending with last st at marker-A; pm between first
and second sts of 71 (81, 99) just picked up.

Both liners:
There are 70 (80, 98) sts along top edge, 2 corner sts
between markers, and 14 vertical placket sts along
ribbing—86 (96, 114) sts total.

LACE PATTERN

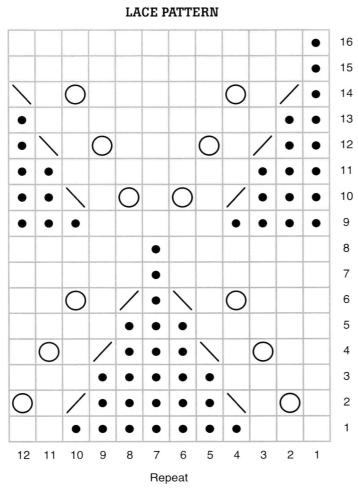

	16
	15
	14
	13
	12
	11
	10
	9
	8
	7
	6
	5
	4
	3
	2
	1

12 11 10 9 8 7 6 5 4 3 2 1

Repeat

Key

☐ Knit

● Purl

╱ K2tog

╲ Ssk

◯ Yo

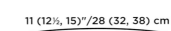

11 (12½, 15)"/28 (32, 38) cm

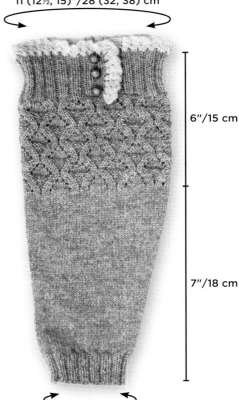

6"/15 cm

7"/18 cm

7 (8, 10)"/18 (20.5, 25.5) cm

Lace Trim

Row 1 (WS): *K1, p1, yo; rep from * to first marker; sl m, p1, yo, p1, sl m; **yo, p1, k1; rep from ** to end—129 (144, 171) sts.

Row 2: *P1, k2; rep from * to first marker; sl m, k3, sl m; **k2, p1; rep from ** to end.

Row 3: *K1, p2, yo; rep from * to first marker; sl m, [p1, yo] twice, p1, sl m; **yo, p2, k1; rep from ** to end—173 (193, 229) sts.

Row 4: *P1, k3; rep from * to first marker; sl m, [k1, p1] twice, k1, sl m; **k3, p1; rep from ** to end.

Row 5: *K1, p3, yo; rep from * to first marker; sl m, p1, yo, k1, p1, k1, yo, p1, sl m; **yo, p3, k1; rep from ** to end—217 (242, 287) sts.

BO all sts using Stretchy BO (see page 6).

Finishing

Weave in ends. Block using Tubular Blocking method (see page 8).

Using tapestry or sewing needle and yarn, sew 3 buttons next to vertical lace, referring to photos for placement.

Lace and Button: Picking Up Stitches Tutorial

These instructions are for picking up stitches for the contrasting lace trim on the right boot liner. The left side is worked similarly, starting with the vertical lace and ending with the horizontal lace.

1. *Horizontal Lace (Lace Edging):* Start 1 st to the left of marker-A on CO edge.

2b. For a total of 71 (81, 99) sts along horizontal edge.

2a. Using B, pick up and knit approximately 3 sts for every 4 sts around.

3. End with last st at marker-A. Pm between last st and next-to-last st.

4. *Vertical Lace (Faux Placket Lace):* In column of sts between marker-A and marker-B, pick up 15 sts (3 stitches for every 4 rows), ending with last st in marker-B. Pm between first and second sts of 15 just picked up.

For the left cuff pick up stitches in the opposite direction, starting at the base of the vertical lace at marker-B, and continue picking up to the top of the cuff, then pick up horizontal lace stitches, placing markers on either side of 2 corner stitches, same as for the right cuff.

6. Work lace trim.

5. There are 70 (80, 98) sts along top edge, 2 corner sts between markers, and 14 vertical placket stitches along ribbing—86 (96, 114) sts total.

Welly Warmers

Welly warmers have a cuff that folds over the top of the boot. These designs are shown with "wellies," or rubber rain boots, but they could be worn with leather boots as well. Typically, this style goes with a straight-shaft boot that may or may not fit tightly around the calf. The fit of the welly warmer is not as tight and conforms more to the boot than the leg, so there are 2 sizing options available instead of 3, like with the tall boot liners.

   Welly warmers are worn with the cuff folded over the top of the boot, so when the cuff is not folded the RS of the cuff faces the same direction as the WS of the leg.

Reversing Sides for Welly Warmers

Because of the fold-over cuff, if you were to work the leg in the same direction as the cuff, you would be working in Reverse Stockinette stitch, which means purling every round. Reversing the sides allows you to knit the leg of the welly warmer instead of purling by working in the opposite direction, but you need to perform a wrap and turn in order to avoid a small hole by the first stitch.

Complete the cuff and the last round of ribbing.

Turn the piece inside out—you will now be working in the opposite direction.

Bring the working yarn to the front, if it is not already there.

Slip the first st of the new round on the RH needle purlwise to the LH needle.

Then bring the yarn to the back.

Slip the first st on the LH needle back to the RH needle (you can place marker in this st to denote "wrapped st").

Insert the RH needle into the wrapped st (first st on the left needle) and knit the wrap and the wrapped st together. Place marker to denote the beginning of round.

Knit the round to the wrapped st.

Hide the wrap by picking up the wrap from front to back with the RH needle.

Colorblock Rib

FINISHED MEASUREMENTS

15"/38 cm tall and 14 (16)"/35.5 (40.5) cm top circumference of cuff

YARN

Color A: 290 (330) yds/265 (302) m worsted weight #5 yarn (shown in Natural Heather, Lion Brand Wool-Ease; 80% acrylic, 20% wool; 197 yds/180 m per 3 oz/85 g skein)

Color B: 50 (55) yds/45.5 (50.5) m worsted weight #5 yarn (shown in Mustard, Lion Brand Wool-Ease; 80% acrylic, 20% wool; 197 yds/180 m per 3 oz/85 g skein)

NEEDLES

☙ US size 6 (4 mm), 1 set of double-pointed needles
☙ US size 7 (4.5 mm), 1 set of double-pointed needles
Adjust needle sizes if necessary to obtain correct gauge.

NOTIONS

☙ Tapestry needle
☙ Stitch marker

GAUGE

Using larger needles, 24 sts and 32 rows in St st = 4"/10 cm, blocked.

Using smaller needles, 24 sts and 36 rows in Offset Rib = 4"/10 cm, blocked and stretched lightly.

LEVEL OF DIFFICULTY

Easy

PATTERN NOTES

☙ Worked in the round from the top down.

PATTERN STITCHES

3 x 3 Rib (multiple of 6 sts)
Pat rnd: *P3, k3; rep from * around.

Offset Rib (multiple of 3 sts)
Rnd 1: K1, p1, *k2, p1; rep from * to last st, k1.
Rnd 2: *P2, k1; rep from * around.
Rep Rnds 1 and 2 for pat.

2 x 2 Rib (multiple of 4 sts)
Pat rnd: *P2, k2; rep from * around.

Welly Warmers

Ribbed Cuff

Using smaller needles and B, CO 84 (96) sts. Mark beg of rnd and join, taking care not to twist sts.
Work 3 rnds in 3 x 3 Rib. Cut B.
Join A and knit for 1 rnd.
Work Offset Rib Pat until piece measures approx 3½"/9 cm from CO edge, ending on Rnd 2.
Do not cut A.

Leg

Join B and knit 1 rnd.

Work 8 rnds in 3 x 3 Rib, carrying A up at beginning of rnd by twisting the 2 yarns together.

Change to larger needles.

Work Reversing Sides technique (see page 84).

Cut B.

With A, knit 2 rnds.

Dec rnd: K1, k2tog, knit to last 3 sts, ssk, k1—2 sts dec'd.

Cont working in St st, rep Dec rnd every 3 (3) rnds 3 (15) more times, then every 4 (4) rnds 14 (5) times—48 (54) sts rem.

Work 16 rnds in 2 x 2 Rib.

BO using Stretchy BO (see page 6).

Finishing

Weave in ends. Block using Tubular Blocking method (see page 8).

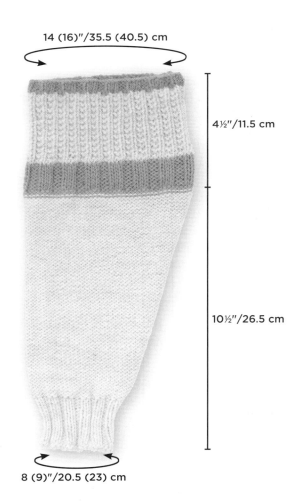

14 (16)"/35.5 (40.5) cm

4½"/11.5 cm

10½"/26.5 cm

8 (9)"/20.5 (23) cm

London

FINISHED MEASUREMENTS
13"/33 cm tall and 15 (17)"/38 (43) cm cuff circumference

YARN
Color A: 55 (65) yds/50.5 (59.5) m fingering weight #1 yarn (shown in Burmese Ruby, Baah La Jolla; 100% superwash merino wool; 400 yds/366 m per 4.1 oz/115 g skein)

Color B: 50 (55) yds/45.5 (50.5) m fingering weight #1 yarn (shown in London Blue, Baah La Jolla; 100% superwash merino wool; 400 yds/366 m per 4.1 oz/115 g skein)

Color C: 15 (20) yds/13.5 (18.5) m fingering weight #1 yarn (shown in Grey Onyx, Baah La Jolla; 100% superwash merino wool; 400 yds/366 m per 4.1 oz/115 g skein)

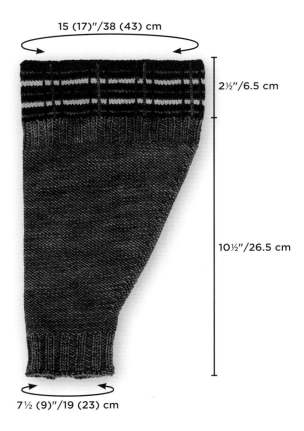

15 (17)"/38 (43) cm

2½"/6.5 cm

10½"/26.5 cm

7½ (9)"/19 (23) cm

Color D: 410 (460) yds/375 (420.5) m DK weight #3 yarn (shown in Obsidian, Baah Sonoma; 100% superwash merino wool; 234 yds/214 m per 3.5 oz/100 g skein)

NEDLES
- US 3 (3.25 mm), 1 set of double-pointed needles
- US 5 (3.75 mm), 1 set of double-pointed needles

Adjust needle sizes if necessary to obtain correct gauge.

NOTIONS
- Tapestry needle
- Stitch marker

GAUGE
Using smaller needles and fingering weight yarn, 32 sts and 40 rows in Plaid Pat = 4"/10 cm square, blocked.

Using larger needles and DK weight yarn, 27 sts and 35 rows in St st = 4"/10 cm square, blocked.

LEVEL OF DIFFICULTY
Intermediate

PATTERN NOTES

❧ Worked from the top down in one piece.
❧ Carry nonworking yarns up at beginning of round by twisting all yarns together.
❧ Vertical lines in Plaid Pat are done using duplicate stitch.

PATTERN STITCH

2 x 2 Rib (multiple of 4 sts)
Pat rnd: *K2, p2; rep from * around.

Welly Warmers

Plaid Cuff

Using smaller needles and A, CO 120 (135) sts. Mark beg of rnd and join, taking care not to twist sts. Do not cut colors until instructed.
Rnds 1–3: *K1, p2, k9, p2, k1; rep from * around.
Rnd 4: With A, knit.
Rnd 5: Join D, knit.
Rnds 6–7: With A, knit.
Rnd 8: Join B, knit.
Rnds 9–10: Join C, knit.
Rnd 11: With B, knit.
Rnds 12–13: With A, knit.
Rnds 14–22: Rep Rnds 5–13.
Rnd 23: With D, knit.
Rnds 24–25: With A, knit.
Cut A, B, and C.

Leg

Change to larger needles.
With D, knit 1 rnd.
Dec rnd: *K3, k2tog; rep from * around—96 (108) sts rem.
Work 9 rnds in 2 x 2 Rib.
Work Reversing Sides technique (see page 84).
Knit 2 rnds.
Dec rnd: K1, k2tog, knit to last 3 sts, ssk, k1—2 sts dec'd.
Cont working in St st, rep Dec rnd every 2 (2) rnds 9 (3) more times, then every 3 (3) rows 14 (18) times—48 (64) sts rem.
Work in St st until piece measures 8½"/21.5 cm from top of Leg section.
Work 14 rnds in 2 x 2 Rib.
BO using Stretchy BO (see page 6).

CUFF COLOR CHART WITH DUPLICATE STITCH

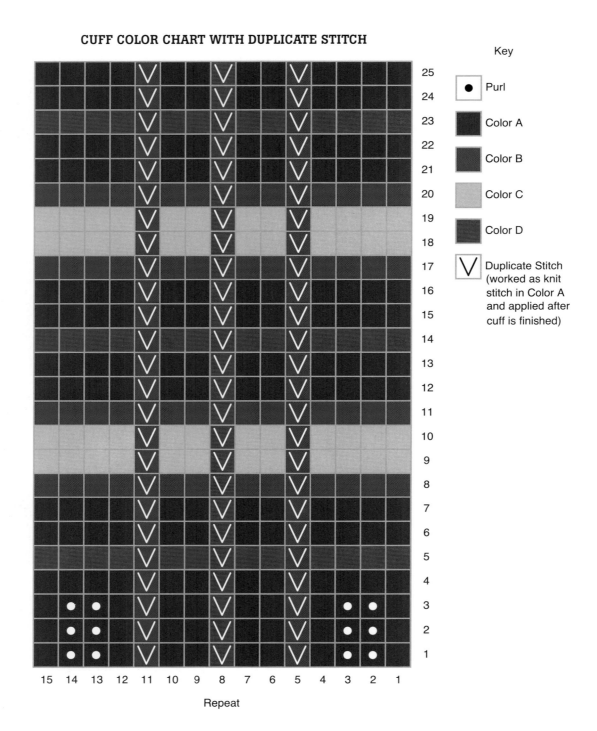

Key

● Purl

■ Color A

■ Color B

■ Color C

■ Color D

V Duplicate Stitch (worked as knit stitch in Color A and applied after cuff is finished)

Repeat

Finishing

Make vertical stripes in Plaid Cuff using Duplicate Stitch (see sidebar on page 93), referring to Cuff Color Chart for placement.

Weave in ends. Block using Tubular Blocking method (see page 8).

Duplicate Stitch Tutorial

In plaid stitch patterns, if you were to knit the vertical lines you would have to use Intarsia technique, which would require a separate portion of yarn for every stripe. Duplicate stitch enables you to add the vertical lines in after knitting by replicating knit stitches using a tapestry needle and yarn.

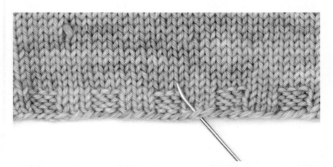

1. Start with about 24" of yarn threaded on to a tapestry needle. With the needle positioned on the WS, bring needle tip up at bottom of the V of your starting knit stitch.

2. Pull the needle through, leaving a short tail to be woven in later.

3. Position needle under the two legs of the V of the stitch above.

4. Pull the needle through.

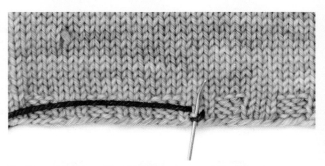

5. Place the needle in at the base of the V where you started in Step 2, and out at the base of the V of the stitch above it.

6. Pull yarn through, and you have now completed a knit stitch.

7. Continue working Steps 3–7, ending the last stitch by pulling yarn through the bottom of the V, leaving the yarn on the WS, cutting and weaving the tail in.

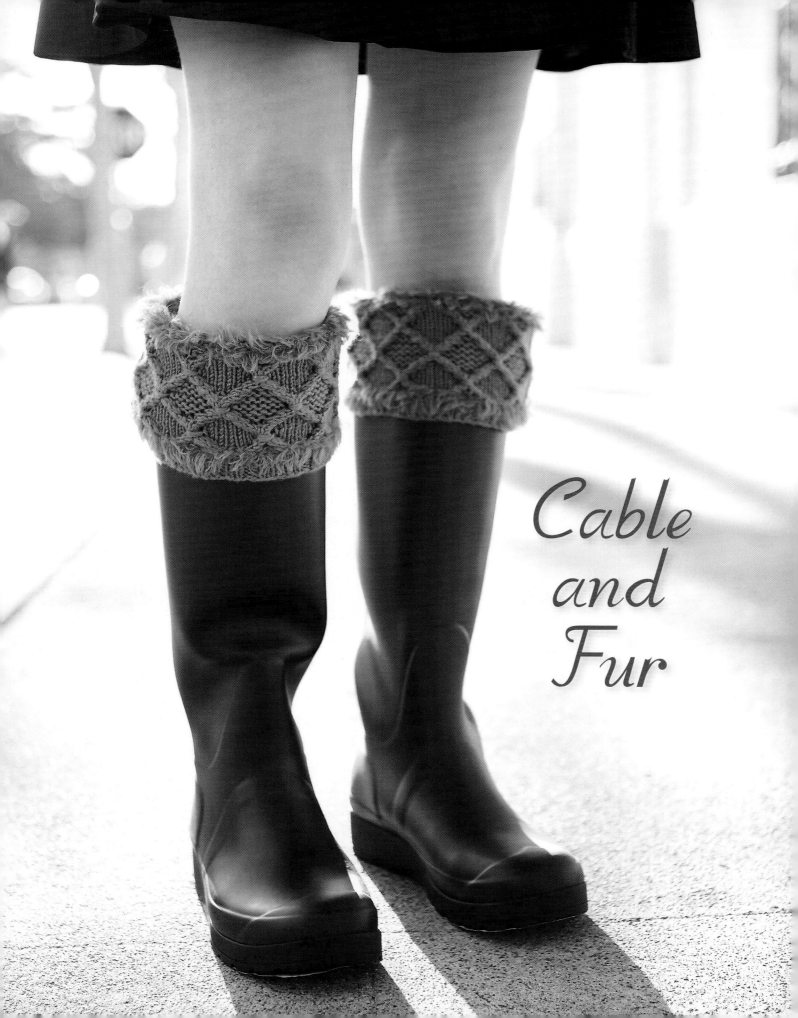

Cable and Fur

FINISHED MEASUREMENTS

15"/38 cm tall and 14 (17)"/35.5 (43) cm cuff circumference

YARN

Yarn A: 350 (480) yds/320 (439) m worsted weight #5 yarn (shown in #305 Dark Grey, Plymouth Yarn Arequipa Worsted; 90% superwash merino, 10% mulberry silk; 218 yds/200 m per 3.5 oz/100 g skein)

Yarn B: 20 (25) yds/18.5 (23) m bulky weight #6 yarn (shown in #205 Dark Grey, Plymouth Yarn Arequipa Fur; 59% baby alpaca, 41% fine merino wool; 65 yds/60 m per 1.8 oz/50 g skein)

NEEDLES

☙ US 7 (4.5 mm), 1 set of double-pointed needles
☙ US 9 (5.5 mm), 1 set of double-pointed needles
Adjust needle sizes if necessary to obtain correct gauge.

NOTIONS

☙ Tapestry needle
☙ Stitch marker
☙ Cable needle

GAUGE

Using smaller needles, 31 sts and 36½ rows in Cable Pat = 4"/10 cm square, blocked.
Using smaller needles, 23 sts and 30 rows in St st = 4"/10 cm square, blocked.

LEVEL OF DIFFICULTY

Intermediate

PATTERN NOTES

☙ Worked from the top down in one piece.
☙ Carry nonworking yarn up at beginning of round by twisting both yarns together.

SPECIAL STITCHES

Cluster (CL): Slip 6 sts to cn; wrap yarn clockwise around sts on cn 3 times; knit the sts from cn.
2/2 RC: Sl 2 sts to cn and hold in back; k2; k2 from cn.
2/2 LC: Sl 2 sts to cn and hold in front; k2; k2 from cn.

PATTERN STITCHES

2 x 2 Rib (multiple of 4 sts)
Pat rnd: *K2, p2; rep from * around.

Cable Pattern (multiple of 12 sts)
Rnd 1: *K1, 2/2 LC, k2, 2/2 RC, k1; rep from * around.
Rnd 2: *K5, p2, k5; rep from * around.
Rnd 3: *K2, 2/2 LC, 2/2 RC, k2; rep from * around.
Rnd 4: Knit.
Rnd 5: *K3, CL, k3; rep from * around.
Rnd 6: Knit.
Rnd 7: *K2, 2/2 RC, 2/2 LC, k2; rep from * around.
Rnd 8: Rep Rnd 2.
Rnd 9: *K1, 2/2 RC, k2, 2/2 LC, k1; rep from * around.
Rnd 10: *K4, p4, k4; rep from * around.
Rnd 11: *2/2 RC, k4, 2/2 LC; rep from * around.
Rnd 12: *K3, p6, k3; rep from * around.
Rnd 13: Sl 3, k6, *CL, k6; rep from * to last 3 sts, CL last 3 sts of Rnd 13 and first 3 sts of Rnd 14.
Rnd 14: [Following CL] P6, k3, *k3, p6, k3; rep from * around.
Rnd 15: *2/2 LC, k4, 2/2 RC; rep from * around.
Rnd 16: Rep Rnd 10.
Rnds 17-25: Rep Rnds 1–9.

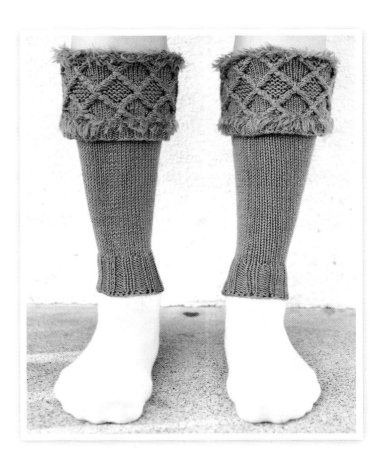

Welly Warmers

Cable Cuff

Using smaller needles and A, CO 80 (100) sts. Mark beg of rnd and join, taking care not to twist sts.

Work 5 rnds in 2 x 2 Rib. Do not cut A.

Using larger needles, join B.

Smaller size only:

Dec rnd: *K1, k2tog; rep from * to last 2 sts, k2—54 sts rem.

Larger size only:

Dec rnd: *K1, k2tog; rep from * to last 4 sts, k2tog twice—66 sts rem.

Both sizes:

Purl for 2 rnds. Cut B.

Switch to smaller needles and A.

Inc rnd: *Kf&b; rep from * around—108 (132) sts.

Work Rnds 1–25 of Cable Pat. Do not cut A.

Using larger needles, join B.

Dec rnd: *K2tog; rep from * around—54 (66) sts.

Purl for 3 rnds. Cut B.

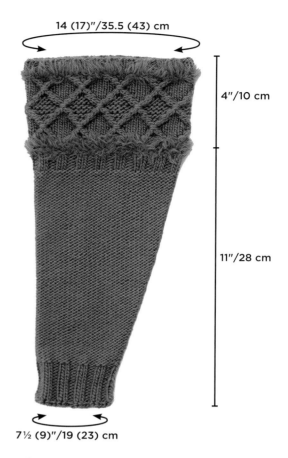

14 (17)"/35.5 (43) cm

4"/10 cm

11"/28 cm

7½ (9)"/19 (23) cm

Smaller size only:

Inc rnd: *K3, kf&b; rep from * to last 2 sts, k1, kf&b—68 sts.

Larger size only:

Inc rnd: *K3, kf&b, k2, kf&b, k3, kf&b; rep from * around—84 sts.

Leg

Both sizes:

Work 5 rnds in 2 x 2 Rib.

Work Reversing Sides technique (see page 84).

Knit 1 rnd.

Dec rnd: K1, k2tog, knit to last 3 sts, ssk, k1—2 sts dec'd.

Cont working in St st, rep Dec rnd every 4 (3) rnds 9 (3) more times, then every 5 (4) rows 4 (12) times—40 (52) sts rem.

Work in St st until piece meas 9"/23 cm from top of Leg section.

Work 14 rnds in 2 x 2 Rib.

BO using Stretchy BO (see page 6).

Finishing

Weave in ends. Block using Tubular Blocking method (see page 8).

CABLE PATTERN

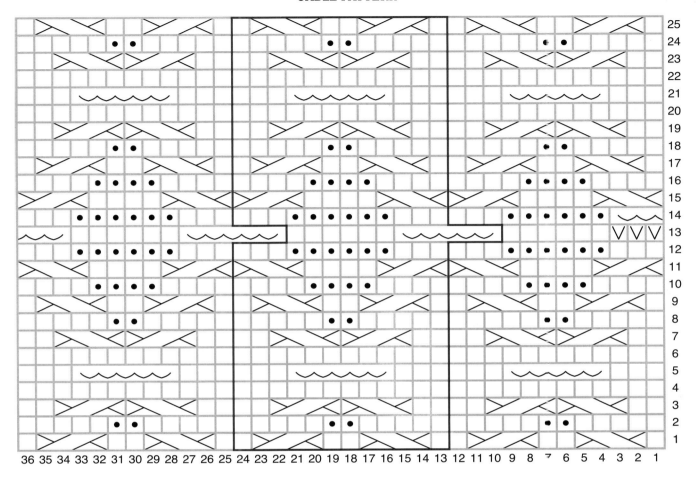

Key

☐	Knit
⊡	Purl
Ⅴ	Slip
▭	2/2 RC
▭	2/2 LC
∼∼∼	CL: Cluster
∼∼	CL last 3 sts of Rnd 13 with first 3 sts of Rnd 14
∼∼	CL last 3 sts of Rnd 13 with first 3 sts of Rnd 14
☐	pattern repeat

Gateway

FINISHED MEASUREMENTS

15"/38 cm tall and 14½ (16½)"/37 (42) cm cuff circumference

YARN

Color A: 280 (305) yds/256 (279) m worsted weight #4 yarn (shown in #152 Oxford Grey, Lion Brand Wool-Ease; 80% acrylic, 20% wool; 197 yds/180 m per 3 oz/85 g skein)

Color B: 20 (25) yds/18.5 (23) m worsted weight #4 yarn (shown in #104 Blush Heather, Lion Brand Wool-Ease; 80% acrylic, 20% wool; 197 yds/180 m per 3 oz/85 g skein)

Color C: 20 (25) yds/18.5 (23) m worsted weight #4 yarn (shown in #98 Natural Heather, Lion Brand Wool-Ease; 80% acrylic, 20% wool; 197 yds/180 m per 3 oz/85 g skein)

NEEDLES

❧ US 7 (4.5 mm), 1 set of double-pointed needles

Adjust needle size if necessary to obtain correct gauge.

NOTIONS

❧ Tapestry needle
❧ Stitch markers
❧ Eight ½" buttons
❧ Sewing needle and thread

GAUGE

23 sts and 31 rows in St st = 4"/10 cm square, blocked

LEVEL OF DIFFICULTY

Intermediate

PATTERN NOTES

❧ Striped cuff worked flat with ribbing on top edge from stitches picked up along side edge.
❧ Leg worked from stitches picked up on opposite side edge.
❧ Faux button placket sewn shut with decorative buttons (no buttonholes).
❧ Carry nonworking yarns on cuff up at beginning of row by twisting all yarns together.

PATTERN STITCH
2 x 2 Rib (multiple of 4 sts)
Pat rnd: *K2, p2; rep from * around.

Welly Warmers

Striped Cuff

Using A, CO 18 sts. Do not cut colors until instructed.
Set-up row (WS): P2, *k2, p2; rep from * around.
Row 1 (RS): K2, *p2, k2; rep from * around.
Row 2: P2, *k2, p2; rep from * around.
Row 3: Rep Row 1, placing markers in first and last sts.
Row 4: Purl.
Row 5: Join B, knit.
Row 6: Purl.
Row 7: With A, knit.
Row 8: Purl.
Rows 9–12: Rep Rows 5–8.
Row 13: Join C, knit.
Row 14: Purl.
Row 15: With A, knit.
Row 16: Purl.
Rows 17–20: Rep Rows 13–16.
Rep Rows 5–20 until piece measures approx 14 (16)"/ 35.5 (40.5) cm, ending on Row 12.
Cut B and C.
With A, knit 3 rows.
BO all sts.

Assemble Cuff

Line up BO edge between markers on WS of cuff, forming a tube, and sew along edge using whipstitch.

Top Ribbing (refer to diagram on page 101)

Left side only:
Holding cuff RS facing, with CO edge to the left, starting in the center of ribbed section, pick up and knit 80 (92) sts (approx 3 sts for every 4 rows) around top of cuff with A, going through both layers of placket.
Mark beg of rnd and join.
Work 2 rnds in 2 x 2 Rib.
BO loosely in pat.

Right side only:
Holding cuff RS facing, with CO edge to the right, starting in the center of ribbed section, pick up and knit 80 sts (approx 3 sts for every 4 rows) around top of cuff with A.
Mark beg of rnd and join.
Work in 2 x 2 Rib for 2 rnds.
BO loosely in pat.

Leg

Both sides:
Holding cuff RS facing, starting in the center of the ribbed section on the opposite side of the cuff, pick up and knit 80 sts (approx 3 sts for every 4 rows) around top of cuff with A.
Work 6 rnds in 2 x 2 Rib.
Work Reversing Sides technique (see page 84).
Knit 2 rnds.
Left side only:
Place marker after 18 sts.
Right side only:
Place marker after 58 sts.

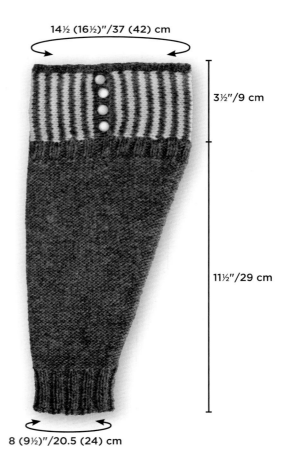

14½ (16½)"/37 (42) cm

3½"/9 cm

11½"/29 cm

8 (9½)"/20.5 (24) cm

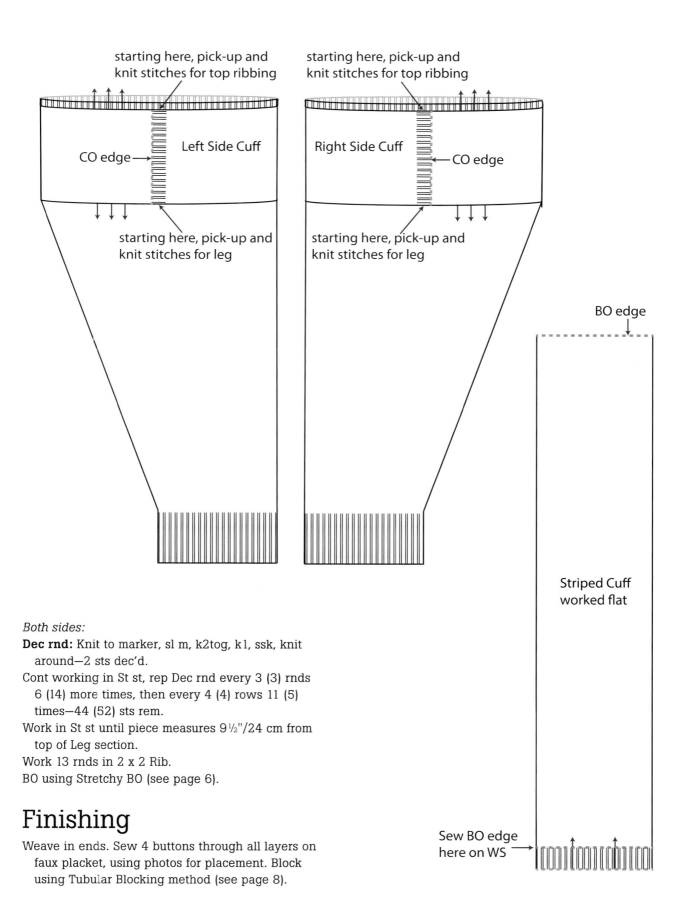

starting here, pick-up and knit stitches for top ribbing

starting here, pick-up and knit stitches for top ribbing

CO edge →

Left Side Cuff

Right Side Cuff

← CO edge

starting here, pick-up and knit stitches for leg

starting here, pick-up and knit stitches for leg

BO edge

Striped Cuff worked flat

Sew BO edge here on WS →

Both sides:

Dec rnd: Knit to marker, sl m, k2tog, k1, ssk, knit around—2 sts dec'd.

Cont working in St st, rep Dec rnd every 3 (3) rnds 6 (14) more times, then every 4 (4) rows 11 (5) times—44 (52) sts rem.

Work in St st until piece measures 9½"/24 cm from top of Leg section.

Work 13 rnds in 2 x 2 Rib.

BO using Stretchy BO (see page 6).

Finishing

Weave in ends. Sew 4 buttons through all layers on faux placket, using photos for placement. Block using Tubular Blocking method (see page 8).

Leg Warmers

Leg warmers are not necessarily designed to be worn with boots, so they have decorative elements that go from the calf to the ankle. Some of these are tapered and some are knit in a very stretchy rib pattern.

I had a lot of fun designing these pieces to be worn with more adventurous outfits. I love the look of leg warmers with Oxfords and over-the-shoe spats with wingtip pumps. Even if you are not a ballerina like my daughter Claire, who modeled the Pirouette leg warmers, I hope you channel your inner dancer and wear these while lounging around the house.

Donegal

FINISHED MEASUREMENTS

16"/40.5 cm tall and 9½ (12½, 16)"/24 (32, 40.5) cm circumference

YARN

305 (405, 515) yds/279 (370.5, 471) m light worsted weight #3 yarn (shown in Aran Tweed, Patons Classic Wool Worsted; 100% wool; 210 yds/192 m per 3.5 oz/100 g skein)

NEEDLES

❧ US size 6 (4 mm), 1 set of double-pointed needles
Adjust needle size if necessary to obtain correct gauge.

NOTIONS

❧ Tapestry needle
❧ Stitch marker

GAUGE

22½ sts and 35 rows in Patterns 1, 2, and 3 = 4"/10 cm square, blocked

LEVEL OF DIFFICULTY

Easy

PATTERN NOTES

❧ Worked in one piece from the bottom up.
❧ Ribbed cuffs on both ends; one end is double the length, to be folded over when worn.

PATTERN STITCHES

2 x 2 Rib (multiple of 4 sts)
Pat rnd: *K2, p2; rep from * around.

Pattern 1 (multiple of 4 sts)
Rnds 1 and 2: Purl.
Rnds 3 and 4: Knit.
Rnds 5–8: Purl.
Rnds 9 and 10: Knit.
Rnds 11 and 12: Purl.
Rep Rnds 1–12 for pat.

Pattern 2 (multiple of 4 sts)
Rnd 1: Knit.
Rnd 2: *K1, p3; rep from * around.
Rnds 3–12: Rep Rnds 1 and 2.
Rnd 13: Knit.
Rep Rnds 1–13 for pat.

(continued on page 107)

Pattern 3 (multiple of 8 sts)
Rnds 1 and 2: Knit.
Rnd 3: *P4, k4; rep from * around.
Rnds 4–6: Knit.
Rnd 7: *K4, p4; rep from * around.
Rnds 8–10: Knit.
Rnd 11: *P4, k4; rep from * around.
Rnds 12 and 13: Knit.
Rep Rnds 1–13 for pat.

Leg Warmers

Ribbed Cuff

CO 48 (64, 80) sts. Mark beg of rnd and join, taking
care not to twist sts.
Work in 2 x 2 Rib for 1 ½"/4 cm.

Pattern Section

Purl for 2 rnds.
Work 13 rnds of Pattern 3.
Work 12 rnds of Pattern 1.
Work 13 rnds of Pattern 2.
Work 12 rnds of Pattern 1.
Work 13 rnds of Pattern 3.
Work 12 rnds of Pattern 1.
Work 13 rnds of Pattern 2.
Purl for 2 rnds.

Ribbed Cuff

Work in 2 x 2 Rib for 3"/7.5 cm.
BO using Stretchy BO (see page 6).

Finishing

Weave in ends. Block using Tubular Blocking
method (see page 8).

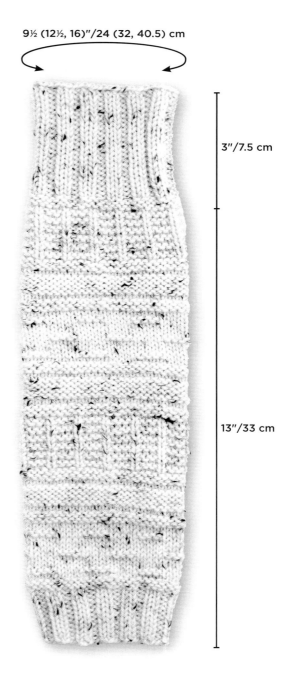

9½ (12½, 16)"/24 (32, 40.5) cm

3"/7.5 cm

13"/33 cm

Stonybreck

FINISHED MEASUREMENTS
15"/38 cm tall and 11 (13, 14½)"/28 (33, 37) cm top circumference

YARN
Color A: 370 (435, 485) yds/338.5 (398, 443.5) m fingering weight #1 yarn (shown in Charcoal, SweetGeorgia Tough Love Sock; 80% superwash merino wool, 20% nylon; 425 yds/388 m per 4.1 oz/115 g skein)

Color B: 45 (50, 55) yds/41 (45.5, 50.5) m fingering weight #1 yarn (shown in Birch, SweetGeorgia Tough Love Sock; 80% superwash merino wool, 20% nylon; 425 yds/388 m per 4.1 oz/115 g skein)

Color C: 35 (40, 45) yds/32 (36.5, 41) m fingering weight #1 yarn (shown in Tumbled Stone, SweetGeorgia Tough Love Sock; 80% superwash merino wool, 20% nylon; 425 yds/388 m per 4.1 oz/115 g skein)

Color D: 20 (20, 25) yds/18.5 (18.5, 23) m fingering weight #1 yarn (shown in Hush, SweetGeorgia Tough Love Sock; 80% superwash merino wool, 20% nylon; 425 yds/388 m per 4.1 oz/115 g skein)

Color E: 25 (30, 35) yds/23 (27.5, 32) m fingering weight #1 yarn (shown in Black Plum, SweetGeorgia Tough Love Sock; 80% superwash merino wool, 20% nylon; 425 yds/388 m per 4.1 oz/115 g skein)

NEEDLES
❦ US 1 (2.25 mm), 1 set of double-pointed needles
❦ US 2 (2.75 mm), 1 set of double-pointed needles
Adjust needle sizes if necessary to obtain correct gauge.

NOTIONS
❦ Tapestry needle
❦ Stitch marker

GAUGE
Using larger needles, 35 sts and 39 rnds in 2-color stranded St st = 4"/10 cm square, blocked.
Using smaller needles, 35 sts and 46 rnds in St st = 4"/10 cm square, blocked.

LEVEL OF DIFFICULTY
Intermediate

PATTERN NOTES
❦ Worked from the top down in one piece.
❦ Colorwork is worked using 2-color stranded St st (see page 31).
❦ Carry nonworking yarn up at beginning of color rounds by twisting yarns together.

PATTERN STITCH
1 x 1 Rib (multiple of 2 sts)
Pat rnd: *K1, p1; rep from * around.

Leg Warmers

Ribbed Cuff

Using smaller needles and A, CO 96 (112, 128) sts.
  Mark beg of rnd and join, taking care not to twist
  sts.
Work 10 rnds in 1 x 1 Rib. Do not cut A.
Knit 1 rnd.

Fair Isle Section

Change to larger needles.
Rnds 1–52: Work 6 (7, 8) reps of Color Pat chart,
  knitting all sts in colors indicated, using all 5 colors,
  working 2 colors per rnd, carrying nonworking
  yarns up at beginning of rnd by twisting the yarns
  together.
Cut all colors except A.

COLOR PATTERN CHART

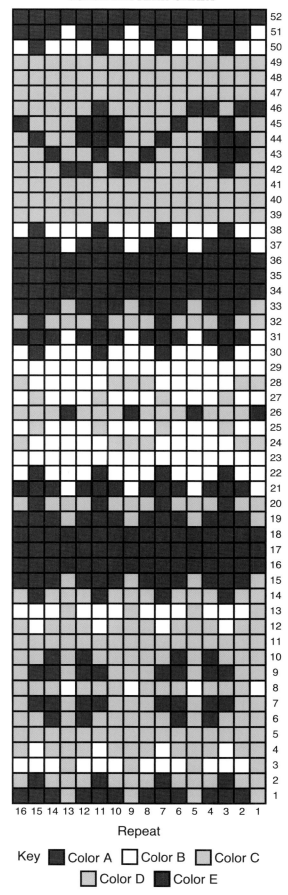

| 52 |
| 51 |
| 50 |
| 49 |
| 48 |
| 47 |
| 46 |
| 45 |
| 44 |
| 43 |
| 42 |
| 41 |
| 40 |
| 39 |
| 38 |
| 37 |
| 36 |
| 35 |
| 34 |
| 33 |
| 32 |
| 31 |
| 30 |
| 29 |
| 28 |
| 27 |
| 26 |
| 25 |
| 24 |
| 23 |
| 22 |
| 21 |
| 20 |
| 19 |
| 18 |
| 17 |
| 16 |
| 15 |
| 14 |
| 13 |
| 12 |
| 11 |
| 10 |
| 9 |
| 8 |
| 7 |
| 6 |
| 5 |
| 4 |
| 3 |
| 2 |
| 1 |

16 15 14 13 12 11 10 9 8 7 6 5 4 3 2 1

Repeat

Key ■ Color A □ Color B ▨ Color C
    ▤ Color D ■ Color E

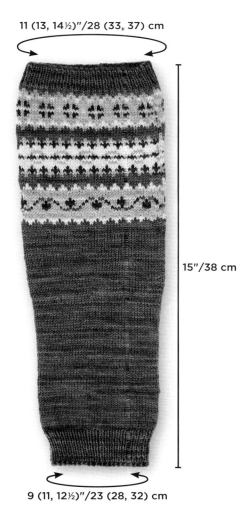

11 (13, 14½)"/28 (33, 37) cm

15"/38 cm

9 (11, 12½)"/23 (28, 32) cm

Leg

Change to smaller needles.

Knit 2 rnds.

Dec rnd: *K10 (12, 14), k2tog; rep from * around—88 (104, 120) sts.

Work in St st until piece measures 8½"/21.5 cm from CO edge.

Dec rnd: *K9 (11, 13), k2tog; rep from * around—80 (96, 112) sts.

Work in St st until piece measures 13½"/35.5 cm from CO edge.

Work 15 rnds in 1 x 1 Rib.

BO using Stretchy BO (see page 6).

Finishing

Weave in ends. Block using Tubular Blocking method (see page 8).

Pirouette

FINISHED MEASUREMENTS

24"/61 cm tall and 8 (10, 12)"/20.5 (25.5, 30.5) cm circumference

YARN

565 (705, 845) yds/516.5 (644.5, 772.5) m sport weight #4 yarn (shown in #516 Petal Pink, Blue Sky Alpaca Sport Weight; 100% baby alpaca; 110 yds/100 m per 1.8 oz/50 g skein)

NEEDLES

❦ US 3 (3.25 mm), 1 set of double-pointed needles
Adjust needle size if necessary to obtain correct gauge.

NOTIONS

❦ Tapestry needle
❦ Stitch markers
❦ Cable needle

GAUGE

38 sts and 36 rows in 2 x 2 Rib = 4"/10 cm square, blocked and unstretched

LEVEL OF DIFFICULTY

Intermediate

PATTERN NOTES

❦ Worked from the top down in one piece.
❦ Split heel worked by binding off stitches mid-round, then casting on stitches in following round.
❦ Cable patterns are reversed in Side 1 and Side 2. Both versions have the same fit, so they are not right and left sides.

SPECIAL STITCHES

2/2 RC: Sl 2 sts to cn and hold in back; k2; k2 from cn.
2/2 RPC: Sl 2 sts to cn and hold in back; k2; p2 from cn.
2/2 LC: Sl 2 sts to cn and hold in front; k2; k2 from cn.
2/2 LPC: Sl 2 sts to cn and hold in front; p2; k2 from cn.

PATTERN STITCHES

1 x 3 Rib (multiple of 4 sts)
Pat rnd: *K1, p3; rep from * around.

2 x 2 Rib (multiple of 4 sts)
Pat rnd: *K2, p2; rep from * around.

Right-Leaning Cable (worked over 16 sts)
Rnd 1: [K2, p2] twice, k2, 2/2 RC, p2.
Rnd 2: [K2, p2] twice, k6, p2.
Rnd 3: [K2, p2] twice, 2/2 RPC, k2, p2.
Rnd 4: [K2, p2] 4 times.
Rnd 5: K2, p2, k2, 2/2 RC, p2, k2, p2.
Rnd 6: K2, p2, k6, p2, k2, p2.
Rnd 7: K2, p2, 2/2 RPC, [k2, p2] twice.
Rnd 8: Rep Rnd 4.
Rnd 9: K2, 2/2 RC, [p2, k2] twice, p2.
Rnd 10: K6, [p2, k2] twice, p2.
Rnd 11: 2/2 RPC, [k2, p2] 3 times.
Rnd 12: Rep Rnd 4.
Rnds 13–24: Repeat Rnds 1–12.

(continued on page 115)

Left-Leaning Cable (worked over 16 sts)

Rnd 1: 2/2 LC, [k2, p2] 3 times.
Rnd 2: K6, [p2, k2] twice, p2.
Rnd 3: K2, 2/2 LPC, [p2, k2] twice, p2.
Rnd 4: [K2, p2] 4 times.
Rnd 5: K2, p2, 2/2 LC, [k2, p2] twice.
Rnd 6: K2, p2, k6, p2, k2, p2.
Rnd 7: K2, p2, k2, 2/2 LPC, p2, k2, p2.
Rnd 8: Rep Rnd 4.
Rnd 9: [K2, p2] twice, 2/2 LC, k2, p2.
Rnd 10: [K2, p2] twice, k6, p2.
Rnd 11: [K2, p2] twice, k2, 2/2 LPC, p2.
Rnd 12: Rep Rnd 4.
Rnds 13–24: Rep Rnds 1–12.

Leg Warmers

Side 1

CO 76 (96, 112) sts. Mark beg of rnd and join, taking care not to twist sts.

Work 7 rnds in 1 x 3 Rib.

Work 2 rnds in 2 x 2 Rib.

Rnd 1: Work 32 sts in 2 x 2 Rib, pm, work Right-Leaning Cable over 16 sts, pm, work in 2 x 2 Rib around.

Rnds 2–24: Work in established pat.

Rnd 25: Work in 2 x 2 Rib to marker, sl m, work Left-Leaning Cable over 16 sts, sl m, work in 2 x 2 Rib around.

Rnds 26–48: Work in established pat.

Rep Rnds 1–48, 2 more times.

Rep Rnds 1–24.

Split Heel (See tutorial on page 46.)

Heel BO rnd: Work 25 (21, 17) sts in 2 x 2 Rib, BO 28 (36, 44) sts using Stretchy BO (see page 6), work in 2 x 2 Rib around—48 (60, 68) sts.

Heel CO rnd: Work 25 (21, 17) sts in 2 x 2 Rib, turn; using knitted CO, CO 30 (38, 46) sts; turn, work in 2 x 2 Rib around—78 (98, 114) sts.

Next rnd: Work 24 (20, 16) sts in 2 x 2 Rib, ssk, k1, p2, work 24 (32, 40) sts in 2 x 2 Rib, k1, k2tog, p2, work in 2 x 2 Rib around—76 (96, 112) sts.

Ribbed Foot

Work in 2 x 2 Rib until piece measures 3"/7.5 cm from Heel CO.

BO all sts using Stretchy BO (see page 6).

Side 2

Work the same as for Side 1, only starting with Left-Leaning Cable and replacing Left-Leaning Cable with Right-Leaning Cable and vice versa throughout pattern.

Finishing

Weave in ends. Block using Tubular Blocking method (see page 8).

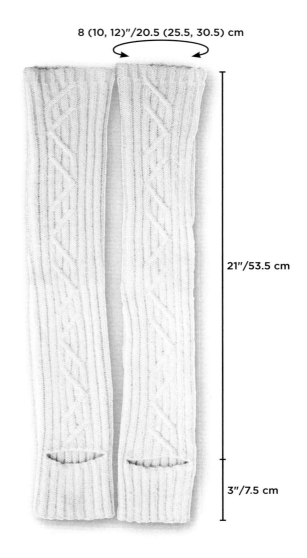

8 (10, 12)"/20.5 (25.5, 30.5) cm

21"/53.5 cm

3"/7.5 cm

RIGHT-LEANING CABLE

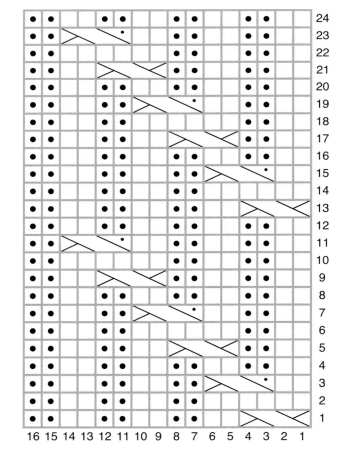

Key

☐	Knit
•	Purl
2/2 RPC	
2/2 RC	

LEFT-LEANING CABLE

Key

☐	Knit
•	Purl
2/2 LPC	
2/2 LC	

Outlander

FINISHED MEASUREMENTS

Leg Warmer: 15½"/39.5 cm tall and 8 (10, 12)"/20.5 (25.5, 30.5) cm top circumference

Corset: 10"/25.5 cm tall and 10 (13, 14½)"/25.5 (33, 37) cm wide (including Lace Scallops)

YARN

Color A (Leg Warmer): 400 (500, 600) yds/366 (457, 548.5) m fingering weight #1 yarn (shown in Magpie, SweetGeorgia Tough Love Sock; 80% superwash merino wool, 20% nylon; 425 yds/388 m per 4.1 oz/115 g skein)

Color B (Corset): 295 (360, 425) yds/269.5 (329, 388.5) m fingering weight #1 yarn (shown in Mink, SweetGeorgia Tough Love Sock; 80% superwash merino wool, 20% nylon; 425 yds/388 m per 4.1 oz/115 g skein)

NEEDLES

* US 1 (2.25 mm), straight needles (small)
* US 2 (2.75 mm), straight and 1 set of double-pointed needles (medium)
* US 3 (3.25 mm), 1 set of double-pointed needles (large)

Adjust needle sizes if necessary to obtain correct gauge.

NOTIONS

* Tapestry needle
* Stitch markers
* 4 yds/3.5 m black satin cording
* Crochet hook and waste yarn (for Provisional Cast-On)

GAUGE

Leg Warmer: Using medium needles, 40 sts and 40 rows in 2 x 3 Rib = 4"/10 cm square, blocked and unstretched.

Corset: Using medium needles, 34 sts and 42½ rows in Herringbone Pat = 4"/10 cm square, blocked.

LEVEL OF DIFFICULTY
Intermediate

PATTERN NOTES
- Garment is in 2 pieces—Leg Warmer with Corset layer laced up over.
- Leg Warmer is worked in one piece in the round from the bottom up.
- Split heel of Leg Warmer is worked by binding off stitches mid-round, then casting on stitches in following round.
- Corset is worked flat and horizontally with two Scalloped Edges worked in separate pieces then joined to Herringbone Section using 3-Needle Bind Off.

SPECIAL STITCHES
M1L (Make 1 Left [Make 1]): Insert LH needle, from front to back, under strand of yarn that runs between next stitch on LH needle and last stitch on RH needle; knit this stitch through back loop. 1 stitch increased.

M1P (Make 1 Purl): Insert LH needle, from front to back, under strand of yarn that runs between next stitch on LH needle and last stitch on RH needle; purl this stitch through back loop. 1 stitch increased.

M1R (Make 1 Right): Insert LH needle, from back to front, under strand of yarn which runs between next stitch on LH needle and last stitch on RH needle; knit this stitch through front loop. 1 stitch increased.

SPECIAL TECHNIQUES
3-Needle Bind-Off: With RS together or facing each other, needles parallel and using a third needle, knit together a stitch from the front needle with one from the back. *Knit together a stitch from the front and back needles, and slip the first stitch over the second to bind off. Repeat from * across, then fasten off last stitch.

Provisional Cast-On: With crochet hook and waste yarn, make a chain several stitches longer than desired cast-on. With knitting needle and project yarn, pick up indicated number of stitches in the "bumps" on back of chain. When indicated in pattern, "unzip" the crochet chain and place live stitches on needle.

PATTERN STITCHES
2 x 3 Rib (multiple of 5 sts)
Pat rnd: K2, *p2, k3; rep from * to last 3 sts, p2, k1.

Lace Pattern (worked in the round over multiple of 10 sts)
Rnd 1: Purl.
Rnd 2: *K1, k2tog, k2, yo, k1, yo, k2, ssk; rep from * around.
Rnd 3: Knit.
Rnd 4: *K1, k2tog, k1, yo, k3, yo, k1, ssk; rep from * around.
Rnd 5: Knit.
Rnd 6: *K1, k2tog, yo, k5, yo, ssk; rep from * around.
Rnd 7: Knit.

Herringbone Pattern (worked flat over multiple of 8 sts plus 4)
Row 1 (RS): K1, p1, *p4, k4; rep from * to last 2 sts, k1, p1.
Row 2: P1, k1, *p3, k4, p1; rep from * to last 2 sts, p1, k1.
Row 3: K1, p1, *k2, p4, k2; rep from * to last 2 sts, k1, p1.
Row 4: P1, k1, *p1, k4, p3; rep from * to last 2 sts, p1, k1.
Row 5: K1, p1, *k4, p4; rep from * to last 2 sts, k1, p1.
Row 6: P1, k1, *k3, p4, k1; rep from * to last 2 sts, p1, k1.
Row 7: K1, p1, *p2, k4, p2; rep from * to last 2 sts, k1, p1.
Row 8: P1, k1, *k1, p4, k3; rep from * to last 2 sts, p1, k1.
Row 9: K1, p1, *k3, p4, k1; rep from * to last 2 sts, k1, p1.
Row 10: P1, k1, *p2, k4, p2; rep from * to last 2 sts, p1, k1.
Row 11: K1, p1, *k1, p4, k3; rep from * to last 2 sts, k1, p1.
Row 12: P1, k1, *p4, k4; rep from * to last 2 sts, p1, k1.
Row 13: K1, p1, *p3, k4, p1; rep from * to last 2 sts, k1, p1.
Row 14: P1, k1, *k2, p4, k2; rep from * to last 2 sts, p1, k1.
Row 15: K1, p1, *p1, k4, p3; rep from * to last 2 sts, k1, p1.
Row 16: P1, k1, *k4, p4; rep from * to last 2 sts, p1, k1.
Rep Rows 1–16 for pat.

Leg Warmers

Foot

Using A and large needles, CO 70 (90, 110) sts. Mark beg of rnd and join, taking care not to twist sts.
Rnds 1–7: Work 7 (9, 11) reps of Lace Pat.
Change to medium needles.
Work in 2 x 3 Rib until piece measures 2½"/6.5 cm.

Split Heel (See tutorial on page 46.)

Heel BO rnd: K2, p1, BO 35 (45, 55) sts using Stretchy BO (see page 6), p1, *k3, p2; rep from * to last st, k1—35 (45, 55) sts.
Heel CO rnd: K2, p1, turn; using knitted CO, CO 37 (47, 57) sts; turn, work in established pat—72 (92, 112) sts.
Next rnd: K2, p2tog, p1 [k3, p2] 6 (8, 10) times, k3, p1, p2tog, *k3, p2; rep from * to last st, k1—70 (90, 110) sts.

Leg

Work 38 rnds in 2 x 3 Rib.
Increase Rounds
Place markers after 20th and 21st sts.
Inc rnd 1: Work in 2 x 3 Rib to first marker, M1R, sl m, k1, sl m, M1L, work in pat around—2 sts inc'd.
Rnds 2–10: Work in established pat, treating inc's as knit sts.
Inc rnd 11: Rep Inc rnd 1.
Rnds 12–20: Work in established pat, treating inc's as knit sts.
Inc rnd 21: Work in pat to first marker, M1P, sl m, k1, sl m, M1P, work in pat around—2 sts inc'd.
Rnds 22–30: Work in established pat, treating inc's as purl sts.
Inc rnd 31: Rep Inc rnd 21.
Rnds 32–40: Work in established pat, treating inc's as purl sts.
Inc rnd 41: Rep Inc rnd 1—80 (100, 120) sts.
Rnd 42: Work in established pat, treating inc's as knit sts.
Work in 2 x 3 Rib until piece measures 14½"/37 cm from CO.
Change to large needles.
Work Rnds 2–7 of Lace Pat.
Knit 1 rnd.
BO all sts loosely using Stretchy BO (see page 6).

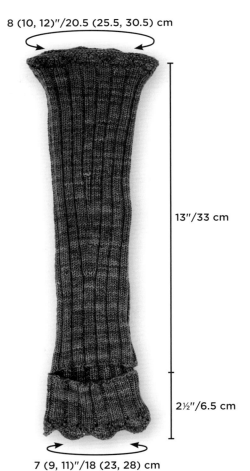

8 (10, 12)"/20.5 (25.5, 30.5) cm

13"/33 cm

2½"/6.5 cm

7 (9, 11)"/18 (23, 28) cm

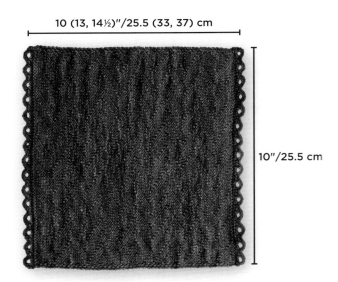

10 (13, 14½)"/25.5 (33, 37) cm

10"/25.5 cm

Corsets

Lace Scallop Edges (make 2)

Using B and small needles, CO 152 sts.

Row 1 (WS): K2, *k1, slip st just worked from RH needle back to LH needle purlwise, with RH needle lift next 7 sts one at a time over this st and off of needle, yo, knit the first st again, k2; rep from *.

Row 2: K1, *p2tog, [k1, p1, k1] in yo, p1; rep from * to last st, k1—77 sts rem.

Row 3: P1, p2tog, purl around—76 sts rem.

Thread tapestry needle with waste yarn and slip sts purlwise on to needle and yarn to be attached later to Herringbone Section; cut A.

Herringbone Section

Using B, crochet hook, and waste yarn, CO 77 sts using Provisional CO.

Next Row: With medium needles and B, p1, p2tog, purl to end—76 sts rem.

Work 9 (11, 13) reps of Herringbone Pat until piece measures approx. 9 (12, 13½)"/23 (30.5, 34.5) cm, ending on Row 16.

Purl 1 row.

Do not BO and do not cut B.

Assemble 2 Lace Scallops to both ends of Herringbone Section as follows.

Place Lace Scallop sts on small needle. Place sts of Herringbone Section on medium needle. With RS together and using a third medium needle and working yarn, join 2 pieces using 3-Needle BO.

Put second Lace Scallop sts on small needle. Unzip Provisional CO of Herringbone Section and place live sts on medium needle. With RS together, join 2 pieces using 3-Needle BO.

Finishing

Weave in ends. Block Leg Warmer using Tubular Blocking method (see page 8). Block Corset flat.

HERRINGBONE PATTERN

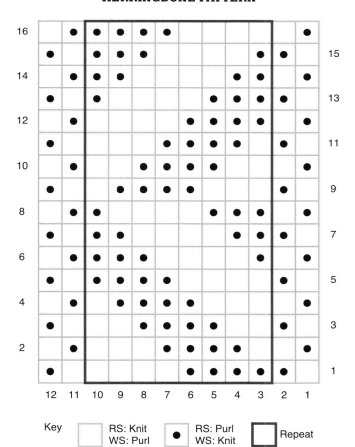

Key | | | RS: Knit WS: Purl | | ● | RS: Purl WS: Knit | | | Repeat

LACE PATTERN

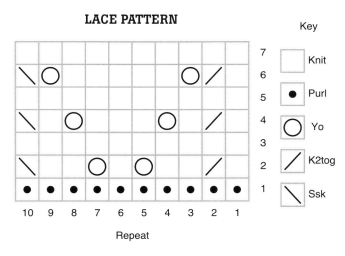

Repeat

Key

Knit

● Purl

○ Yo

／ K2tog

＼ Ssk

Acknowledgments

As always, thank you to my ever-patient family for putting up with all of my crazy creative endeavors. I am forever grateful to my sample knitter, Joan Kass, who beautifully knit many of the pieces in this book and became a great friend along the way. A special thanks to John Fluevog (Fluevog.com) and the fine crew at the Abbot Kinney store for many of the beautiful boots modeled in this book. Chloe, Jewel, and Claire, you made all the designs come to life, and Katie Wong, you made their beauty shine through! Thanks also to Margie Evans, who helped make our photo shoot run seamlessly, and Candi Derr for keeping me honest with your thorough editing. And last but not least, thank you Misty Matz for your keen eye in capturing fun, beautiful, and creative photographs.

Photography: Misty Matz

Sample knitting: Joan Kass

Hair and makeup:
Katie Wong for Theresa Huang Makeup and Hair

Location: Nicole Caldwell Photography Studio
and Old Towne Orange, California

Models: Chloe Evans, Jewel Henderson, Claire Powers

Yarn Sources

Thank you to the following companies who generously provided yarn for the projects in this book:

Baah Yarn, baahyarn.com

Big Bad Wool, bbwool.com

Blue Sky Fibers, blueskyfibers.com

Cascade, cascadeyarns.com

Cloudborn, craftsy.com

Lion Brand Yarns, lionbrand.com

Loops & Threads, michaels.com

Madelinetosh, madelinetosh.com

Patons, yarnspirations.com/patons

Plymouth, plymouthyarn.com

Rowan Yarns, knitrowan.com

SweetGeorgia, sweetgeorgiayarns.com